Volcanic Adventures in Tonga

Species Conservation on Tin Can Island

Ann Göth

Natural Publishing

Volcanic Adventures in Tonga-Species Conservation on Tin Can Island

Copyright © 2023 by Ann Göth

All rights reserved, except under the conditions described in the Australian Copyright Act 1968 and subsequent amendments. No part of this book may be reproduced, distributed, or transmitted in any form or by any means, including photocopying, recording, or other electronic or mechanical methods, without the prior written permission of the publisher, except in the case of brief quotations embodied in critical reviews and certain other noncommercial uses permitted by copyright law.

For permission requests, write to goethann@gmail.com

The stories, the experiences, and the words are the author's alone.

Illustrations ©Ann Göth

Book Cover by Sole from Luna Design

Ann Göth's website: https://anngothauthor.com

First edition published by Austin Macauley Publisher, 2023 (now out of print): ISBN 978-1-035-80951-6 (Paperback); ISBN 978-1-035-80952-3 (e-book)

Second printing by Natural Publishing, 2024:

ISBN 978-0-6486037-5-7 (Paperback); ISBN 978-0-6486037-6-4 (e-book)

This is a reprint of the original edition published in 2023. No significant changes have been made to the content of this book.

A catalogue record for this title is available from the **National Library of Australia** and the **State Library of NSW**.

Foreword

The family of birds known as the megapodes are among the most astonishing and bizarre of all Avian groups. When stories of these species and their behaviour reached Europe in the 18th Century, they were dismissed as fanciful tales from confused explorers. Birds burying their eggs in the sides of volcanoes or building huge mounds? Obviously, exaggerations of over-excited travellers trying to sell books.

When explorers finally investigated these otherwise unremarkable-looking birds, the list of remarkable features continued to grow. Some of these birds did construct enormous mounds of organic matter, which were used as incubation sites, while others abandoned their eggs deep inside volcanoes or hot sand. They were the only birds providing absolutely no parental care for their young, and their hatchlings were so advanced they were the only birds classed as super-precocial, being able to fend for themselves as soon as they hatched. And as the studies have continued, so have the discoveries.

There is a problem, however. Almost everything we know in detail about megapodes comes from just a few species. Apart from the three living in Australia, the other nineteen species occur in remote rainforests and on faraway islands, and they are often secretive and reclusive. Almost everywhere, local people exploit their eggs, and most species are now in decline. The challenges associated with studying most megapodes are formidable. The logistics alone of spending the long periods of time necessary to really understand the lives of these birds in their natural habitats has meant that we know very little about most species. And the more remote they live, the less likely anyone will be motivated to undertake the arduous research required.

This is why *Volcanic Adventures in Tonga* is so compelling. Despite living in Europe, as far from a remote tropical island as possible, Ann Göth became intrigued, possibly even a little obsessed, with these strange birds. While the romantic dream of living on a tiny volcano in the South Pacific inevitably included the promise of adventure and discovery in a spectacular landscape, the reality was very different. In many ways, her experience was both far more challenging and yet far more rewarding than anyone could have expected. Yet, despite the weather, discomfort and exhaustion, the scientific and conservation work Ann was able to complete was extraordinary in its detail and importance. Her discoveries transformed what was known about island-dwelling megapodes and also highlighted their precarious existence. Both local and global threats now bear down on these islands, bringing potentially catastrophic consequences to the wildlife and the people who live their intertwined lives there.

Dr Göth is now an international authority on megapodes, with an impressive resume of scientific publications, including the book we wrote together, *Mound-builders*. Long before PhDs and careful laboratory experiments under strictly controlled conditions, however, there was Ann's remarkable and highly personal origin story. It has all the intrigue, adventure, romance, disappointment, discovery and danger you would expect from one of those breathless traveller's tales of past eras. This time, however, the story is actually true.

Professor Emeritus Darryl Jones, Griffith University, Co-author of *The Megapodes* (Oxford University Press) and *Mound-builders* (CSIRO Publications).

Praise for Volcanic Adventures in Tonga

Ann's exceptional tales of volcanic exploration have been meticulously preserved within the pages of this remarkable book, which undoubtedly deserves a five star rating. Seamlessly blending captivating storytelling with enlightening information, Ann's contagious passion resonates from the first page to the last, creating an immersive experience that will captivate readers seeking an escape to a world both mesmerizing and unforgiving. - **Literary Titan 5-star review**, July 2024

Like any remarkable travel story, her book is an intriguing mix of difficulties and delights... this book was an exciting opportunity for me to learn about the Tongan people. It includes Ann's vivid account of various things that are common to many tribal societies, such as matriarchy and having few material possessions. The reader gets to experience the rich culture of the Tongan people and the beauty of the natural world on the remote island as if in person. I loved that it reveals a Westerner's view of a different culture and the author's honest opinion of the things she found challenging, including language differences and being told that she is not "big fat" enough. Volcanic Adventures in Tonga offers a fun adventure and a profound, memorable travel experience. It's also a timely reminder to preserve endangered species and be conscious of climate change. Every travel enthusiast and conservationist would love this book. I didn't want to miss a thing! – **Foluso Falaye for Readers' Favorite, 5-star review.** September 2024

This is an extraordinary book. If you've ever wanted to know what it might be like, as a Western person, to be marooned on one of the remotest islands of one of the remotest countries in the world, read this story. The complex relationships between the islanders and this couple who stayed for almost two years contain aspects that people who live in developed countries would never imagine. This is as much a story about human interaction and Indigenous culture as it is about volcanoes and saving rare birds. Well written, entertaining and a quick, compelling read. – **Simon Michael Prior, 5-star review, Award-winning travel author.**

The narrative is a joyous delight to read; the author's enthusiasm and devotion to Conservation and Biology is rare in today's cynical and jaded culture!– **Cobwebby Goodreads reviewer, 5-star review.**

This tale goes beyond being a travel memoir and a documentation of a conservation project. In fact, the success of the scientific project becomes a moot point—what shines through Ann's words is the resilience of the human spirit. And what can be accomplished through kindness, understanding, and an open heart that embraces other cultures.- **Clara Fay, 5-star review, Award-winning author.**

A remote Pacific Island, an intriguing and unique species of bird for this young scientist to observe and protect, and a way of life far removed from the everyday as it is possible to get. The scientist and the artist combined to create this entertaining and informative memoir, full of the day-to-day reality of life on a remote island. Full of insightful observations of the Tongan people and their simple way of life, and the unusual species of Malau bird she was tracking, alongside her youthful romance with her partner on the trip, this was a delightful and informative book. Recommended.- **Alyson Sheldrake, 5-star review, Award-winning author.**

Contents

Dedication and Paying Respect	1
Disclaimer	2
15 November 1991	3
1. Enthusiasm and Preparations	5
2. In the City of Love	11
3. Suddenly on the Moana	16
4. Jumping Ashore	20
5. Settling in and a Church Service	23
6. A First Taste of Village Life—and Muttonbirds	26
7. Monster Centipedes	30
8. Finding the Malau	33
9. Culinary Insights	38
10. Head First Deep Down in a Burrow	42
11. Ofato Grubs and Kava	45
12. A Phone Expedition	48
13. Big Fat or Small Fat?	51
14. Volcanic Powers	55
15. Lake on the Islet in the Lake on the Island in the Sea	59

Photos	65
16. Ivo, The Celebrity from the Air	82
17. The Professor and War Day Arrive	86
18. Critters in Oats and an Ear	91
19. Christmas and New Year	94
20. Vava'u and Tofua Volcano	98
21. A Return Trip with Obstacles	109
22. On Late Volcano— Mafana, Mafana!	115
23. Meeting the Minister— In Tongan Time	124
24. Ana e Ivo Malau	126
25. First Translocation to Late Volcano	130
26. You Can Achieve Anything If You Maintain Your Pride!	133
27. A Cyclone at Last	139
28. A Bit Less Pālangi?	146
29. Stuck on Tin Can Island?	149
30. Almost Killed by the King	155
Afterword: Back Home with Updates	162
Afterthought. Life in Tonga Under Climate Change	170
Acknowledgements	174
Maps	176
Places, Names and Tongan Words	179
About the author	183
Further Reading	184

Dedication and Paying Respect

I dedicate this book to Toby and Wayne, the two special men who joined my life many years after I returned from Tonga. May they enjoy reading about my past and the concept of Tongan Time; that is, the prioritising of the present moment over worrying about the future. I also dedicate this book to my mum, who meticulously typed up all the letters I wrote to her from Tonga so many years ago, providing the material that became the foundation of this book.

I am writing this book on the land of the Gadigal people of the Eora nation. In the spirit of reconciliation, I acknowledge the Traditional Custodians of these lands and their connections to land, sea, and community. I pay my respect to their Elders, past and present, and extend that respect to all Aboriginal and Torres Strait Islander peoples today.

I would also like to honour the resilient and noble people of Tonga, and the revered ancestors who have paved the way with their wisdom, courage, and enduring spirit. I pay my respects to their rich heritage and the profound legacy that continues to inspire and guide future generations. May their traditions, stories, and values be forever honoured and cherished.

Disclaimer

All the stories in this book are based on actual events, documented in detailed letters to my parents. I have occasionally adjusted the order of events and combined similar content into a single chapter for readability. In some parts, I have added information about Polynesian culture that was unavailable to me in 1991–1993 but is now accessible through the internet. All the people in this book, past and present, are real. A few individuals permitted me to use their real names, while for others, I have changed the names to protect their privacy.

Malau bird singing

15 November 1991

I am sitting in a bird hide in Tonga, on a volcano that is asleep. Geologists would call it dormant, and they also predict that this volcano will erupt again sometime soon. I am putting aside such sombre thoughts of eruptions—too scary. Instead, I focus on the sounds and sights around me. It's been decades since the volcano last erupted, enabling plants to flourish. It can't get any lusher than this—dense vegetation in all shades of green, with glossy, big leaves typical of tropical plants. A few drops from the last bout of rain are still dripping down on me, and the air is steaming in 80 percent humidity. So close to the equator, it is no wonder my clothes are drenched in sweat, and the frequent daily showers bring welcome cooling relief.

My ears tune in to the sounds around me, but there are few. Silence is what I mainly experience, and even most of the birds seem to be asleep in the midday heat. The occasional 'boo-hoo' of a Pacific pigeon echoes through the forest, but otherwise, there is nothing to hear, apart from mosquitoes buzzing and the wind whistling in the tall ironbark trees. I can't hear my boyfriend preparing corned beef on our campfire, and there are no other people nearby. The closest Polynesians live behind the 200-metre-high crater rim surrounding me, and the next outpost of Western civilisation lies beyond 400 kilometres of Pacific Ocean.

Suddenly, two Malau emerge from the jungle onto a small open area that is barren and covered in loose soil. I don't move a muscle in my bird hide so as not to scare them away, apart from carefully fetching my notebook and pencil to write down my observations. The two birds sing a beautiful duet, with the male starting and the female joining in soon after. She then starts to dig in the loose soil, and within a few minutes, a burrow takes shape, which gradually becomes deep enough to swallow her whole body. With her large feet, she keeps digging and disappears into the hole. The only sign of her presence is the soil that flies out of the entrance in bursts and lands up to one metre from the burrow. Meanwhile, the male carefully watches over her, listening for any signs of predators that may endanger his vulnerable partner down in that burrow. He is watchful until she has completed what she has come to do: lay her one egg that weighs almost a quarter of her body weight. The volcano might be sleepy, but it is still active underground, and she will leave the incubation of her egg to this mighty power. For 60 days, her egg will be warmed by the volcano, enough for a chick to develop and hatch, deep down in that burrow.

This is not how birds usually behave, I know. They don't dig holes like moles and use volcanoes as incubators. But I am not observing any ordinary bird here. Malau are different, very different indeed, and they are the reason why I have come to this remote island on the other side of the world, all the way from Austria. It has taken months of preparation back home, then weeks of settling in and being accepted by the locals, before I can finally make this observation and get a glimpse into the life of a critically endangered and highly unusual bird.

The pair has filled the burrow with soil again and left. Just as I am about to leave my hide, a little head pops up out of that same burrow. Brown, fluffy, and very cute, its body still buried in the soil. The little chick scans its surroundings for dangerous animals that may eat or catch it. It is exhausted from having dug itself out of a 1.5-metre depth, but without any parents to rely on, the young Malau needs to take good care of itself.

1

Enthusiasm and Preparations

It is February 1991, and I will soon turn 21. My mind is set on one thing: I desperately want to contribute to the conservation of endangered animals—somewhere, somehow. As an enthusiastic undergraduate student of biology, I have read distressing stories about species extinction. It is my utmost desire to make a difference.

Out of the blue, my boyfriend Ivo, from Germany, calls to ask whether I would like to join him on a two-year conservation mission to help save an endangered and highly unusual bird on the remote island of Niuafo'ou in Tonga. My response comes quicker than a cannonball: "Yes!" It matters little that I don't know where Tonga is. My home is Austria, and the island kingdom of Tonga, on the other side of the world, was not part of the geography curriculum at school. My childhood revolved around skiing and climbing mountains, not coconut palms.

I am also not concerned that we have no idea how to fund this project or that it could be somewhat challenging to spend two years on a remote island with a boyfriend I have only known for seven months. He, too, is a biology student, and we share a deep interest in the natural world, but our relationship is still young. My enthusiasm and youthful optimism help me overlook such concerns. Although seven months of dating is short, we harmoniously spent last summer at a remote field station in Germany. We lived a simple life in an old building container and studied birds together. While this experience doesn't quite compare to living on a remote island, it's a similar idea.

I can easily envision these seven months with Ivo extending into two years, or even more, without any problems. During our time in the building container, I got to know him as a spirited, passionate, earnest, and yet complex and thoughtful man—the kind of man I could imagine spending two years on an island with. It's not just our interest in all things living that we share, but also a matching sense of humour and physical stamina, both of which are expected to be essential on an expedition like this. Also important is our similar resilience to mental challenges, though Ivo's is probably more developed than mine. He was born and raised in East Germany (German Democratic Republic) behind the Wall and endured horrendous attempts to escape that totalitarian Communist regime before eventually becoming a refugee in West Germany, years before the Wall came down. My upbringing was more stable, but I had to leave home early to attend high school and travelled extensively on my own, off the beaten track, in Ireland and Canada.

What appeals to me most is that if I am accepted for this project, I will have a chance to prove to myself that I can step into the shoes of the explorers and conservationists I so admire, foremost Jane Goodall and Dian Fossey, two inspirational women who survived many hardships to study and protect primates in the field. Will I be able to endure the unavoidable difficulties and deprivations that come with conducting fieldwork in a remote tropical destination?

The adventurer in me has always loved the idea of being part of such an expedition, proving to myself that I can do more than live a comfortable life in Western civilisation, especially if it serves the purpose of saving an endangered species from extinction. It doesn't have to be a primate; a bird will do. After all, I am an avid birdwatcher.

This project will also help me satisfy my curiosity about two of my favourite subjects: ethnology, or the study of human cultures, and island biogeography. I am fascinated by how indigenous people worldwide have established cultures and relationships with nature that are so different from ours. Being part of a remote community in Polynesia seems like a grand opportunity to experience this in person. Island biogeography is exciting because it involves such a large degree of chance, and to me, life is riddled with chance. A favourite quote above my bed reads, 'Life is full of chances; don't miss yours today.' The composition of island fauna and flora is often the result of chance too. An animal or plant clings to some driftwood or is carried by a storm and then, by pure luck, ends up on a tiny stretch of land in a vast ocean to establish a new population there. My approach to life is a bit like that: see where the wind carries me and cling to those opportunities. Living on a remote island for two years seems like an opportunity not to be missed.

Now we need to tackle the task of turning our goodwill into an actual project. The easiest part is finding out where Niuafo'ou is. An atlas quickly tells us that it lies close to the equator—nice and humid—and is the northernmost of 171 scattered islands that make up the Kingdom of Tonga. The tiny dot in the Pacific Ocean measures only 8 kilometres in diameter. It lies 400 kilometres from the next larger island group, Vava'u, and 600 kilometres from Nuku'alofa, the capital of Tonga—a long way across the sea to the nearest comforts of Western civilisation.

Less straightforward is the retrieval of more detailed information about this island. The Internet is still unknown to us, so we visit several libraries instead. The musty smell of library basements, where old reports are only available on microfilm, makes us feel like mummies in a crypt. Microfilms are those small films with scaled-down reproductions of documents that you can only barely read with a special machine. Occasionally, when reading with watery, exhausted eyes for hours, we find our island mentioned in obscure travel reports.

What we discover is slightly alarming. Niuafo'ou is a dormant volcano, meaning it has erupted regularly since at least 1814 and can still erupt at any time. The last recorded eruption occurred in 1946, but there was most likely also a minor one in 1985[1]. Our only consolation is that, so far, eruptions have always occurred in small parts of the island. All inhabitants managed to escape, except for two eruptions in 1814 and 1886, when casualties were reported[2]. The villages are on the outside of the crater, and the people's refuge was the crater rim, which is only 200 metres high because the top cone of the volcano collapsed inward thousands of years ago.

Over the years, rainwater filled the centre of the almost circular island, creating a large crater lake. It is nice to know that we would have a lake to swim in, as the island has no running water, and showers may be a rare commodity. It is also pleasant to discover that the name Niuafo'ou translates into 'New Coconut Land.' We Europeans, who have always associated coconut palms with a faraway tropical paradise, would be excited to go to an island named after them.

The second name for Niuafo'ou is also rather exotic: Tin Can Island. In the late 19th and early 20th centuries, when passing ships carried letters for the 400 islanders, the mail was sealed in tin cans and thrown overboard, about a mile offshore. Like today, the volcanic coast was far too rough for ships to get close to it, so these anchored far offshore. Then, alerted by the hoot of the ship, some strong men swam out to fetch the tin from the sea, day or night, ignoring sharks and currents, before collecting and then delivering the mail to its recipients. Sometimes they struggled for up to six hours to retrieve the tin, and at least one was eaten by a shark. This tradition became well-known and admired,

---

1. Paul Taylor, personal communication

2. Same source as above

especially by passengers on passing cruise liners. As a result, the local post office started issuing and selling its own stamps. These feature the word Niuafo'ou instead of Tonga as the country of origin, and they are now much sought after by stamp collectors worldwide.

So far, we are still thinking of this expedition as a dream because our participation is not yet confirmed. Ivo's supervisor, the Professor, had posted a note about it on his blackboard, which Ivo then read, but we still need to convince this man that we are the people for the job. The Professor, a tall, grey-haired academic in his late 60s, leads this project from the German university where Ivo is enrolled for his Master's degree in Biology. Initially, the Professor firmly rejects the idea that a young woman should be part of such an expedition. After returning several times to his office, we convince the Professor of our enthusiasm, dedication, and knowledge about the project, and finally, the job is ours.

The Professor recently visited a small zoo in Tonga that is funded by a larger German zoo. As a result, he and the small zoo's manager, Mr Hopps, agreed to establish a conservation project for the endangered Malau bird. They decided that the Professor would find students to carry out the project and oversee the preparation of the mission, whereas Mr Hopps, also a German, would support the students within Tonga and apply for research permits and visas. We are glad to hear that we will have a local support person who speaks German, has lived in Tonga for some years and is familiar with Anga Faka-Tonga—the Tongan way of life. From what we have read, this lifestyle is rather different from ours, and we will benefit from having the support of an insider. This fact is also a consolation for my parents, who admit to being a bit worried. They have always encouraged me to follow my adventurous spirit, but maybe they didn't anticipate that, at the age of 21, I would already venture to such a remote place on the other side of the world. Ivo's parents are less concerned. They were more worried when he attempted to escape East Germany than they are now.

A phone call to Mr Hopps sheds some light on the true nature of our mission. The endangered bird's official name is 'Polynesian megapode', its scientific name *Megapodius pritchardii*, but the locals call it Malau. Its fate is closely linked to Niuafo'ou and the volcano, and it is endemic, meaning it nowadays occurs nowhere else in the world. Its future on this one island is uncertain, so conservationists have suggested a translocation of some Malau to another volcanic island, to establish a second population as a safeguard for the future. Scientists who love studying fossil bones have found that this species used to occur on additional islands in the area, but the first Polynesians who settled there ate them and thus most likely contributed to their extinction on all islands except Niuafo'ou.[3] A translocation would thus help restore the original distribution and protect this species from total extinction in the future.

The Malau belongs to a small group of unusual birds called Megapodes, comprising 22 species that occur anywhere between the Nicobar Islands in the West and Tonga in the East. None of them incubate their eggs themselves by sitting on them. Instead, they use external heat sources for incubation. The Australian brush-turkey and malleefowl use the heat produced by rotting vegetation to incubate their eggs, but the Tongan Malau leave the incubation to the volcano. The females bury their eggs in the volcanically heated soil around the crater lake. This burying is the only parental care they provide, as the chicks have to dig themselves out upon hatching deep in the ground. The youngsters live entirely on their own from the moment they hatch, making Malau and all Megapodes the only birds on Earth that are so highly independent and grow up without any care from their parents. They are basically orphans from birth.

One Englishman, David Todd, studied the birds ten years before us, and he published the fact that they are endangered for two reasons. First, a volcanic eruption, as predicted by geologists, could exterminate the population or reduce it to very low numbers. Second, people eat their eggs. Locals know where the birds lay their eggs week after week and year after year. Both men and women have high regard for the strength and stamina of those few men who manage to dig up the eggs from their deep burrows by hand, so the digging serves as both food provisioning and proof of masculinity.

All these factors led to the Malau being declared Critically Endangered by the International Union for the Conservation of Nature. Our first aim will be to determine how many Malau still exist, what threats they face, and study their behaviour and ecology. All of this will better enable us to propose suitable conservation measures. Our second aim will be to survey another uninhabited volcanic island in Tonga and maybe translocate some Malau there, hoping that we will establish a second population.

The Professor and Mr Hopps had the idea for the project, but they do not have the funds. So the task of writing letters to raise money falls to us, whereas our supervisors add credibility to the funding pleas. It is 1991, and the use of desktop computers is in its infancy. Ivo has some experience with the operating system MS-DOS, while I am a computer novice and suffer from considerable anguish when learning how to use this system. Nevertheless, we write many letters to potential funders, often without receiving a reply. Our funding pleas highlight the benefits of our dedication to conservation and

---

3. Steadman, D.W. (2006). *Extinction and Biogeography of Tropical Pacific Birds*. Chicago: University of Chicago Press.

the sustainability of a natural resource in Tonga. Eventually, after five months, we have gathered enough funds to sustain the project for two years. I am thrilled that apart from some larger conservation organisations and companies, a few family friends have also chipped in, as has my dear grandfather, a scientist who has always supported my passion for science.

All that is left to do is gather our equipment and explore our travelling options. It turns out that to get from Germany to Tonga, we can't fly via Asia. This route would be the quickest and cheapest but only allows for 32 kg of luggage per person. So we choose the Western route via the US, as this lets us take twice as much baggage. Our main problem is that no airline offers tickets valid for two years, so we need to buy a one-way ticket. Luckily, our contact, Mr Hopps, confidently assures us that this is okay and that we can enter Tonga without a return ticket because he has applied for a research permit for us. We trust he is correct and that we will indeed be able to obtain a return ticket when we are over there. While I tell my worried parents a lot of details about our project, this lack of a return ticket is one I diligently forget to mention.

Weighing equipment down to the gram becomes our favourite pastime during these next six weeks, while we gather what we think will be needed over two years. Our growing piles of stuff are slowly taking over a basement some friends kindly offer us. Occasionally, Ivo and I argue about what to take, for example, whether we need two or three pencils or if we can afford to take an additional novel as a luxury weight. But overall, we get along well and enjoy the feeling of being real explorers who pack for their big expedition to the tropics.

While spending all these months preparing, I stay with Ivo in his tiny one-room accommodation in a student dorm, which has just enough space to fit our mattress and a table. This intimate and confined existence is a bit of a test for what is to come, and so far, it is going well.

A doctor friend of the family goes out of his way to supply us with a substantial medical kit, including prescription medications, especially when he hears about the absence of a doctor or hospital on the island. We are relieved to know that there is no malaria in Tonga, so that is one problem less to tackle. But the lack of medical services is a detail I also ignore in conversations with my parents. We repack our two waterproof backpack barrels several times until we have filled every square millimetre of space. Finally, in mid-August 1991, we are ready to fly, cheerful and excited. At Frankfurt airport, the flight attendants kindly ignore our unusual hand luggage: three solar panels, which will provide electricity on the island, and a portable incubator for eggs. Maybe our enthusiastic smiles distract them from questioning the weight and dimensions of this baggage.

2

In the City of Love

How can you experience three nights within 30 hours? Fly from Frankfurt to Los Angeles, change planes, land for a pitstop in Hawaii, and continue to Fiji. By the time you reach Hawaii, the nights and days merge. Our sense of time completely vanishes when we cross the dateline shortly before reaching the Fiji Islands, jumping one day ahead—a day we won't reclaim until returning home in two years.

In Fiji, we are supposed to board a flight operated by Air Pacific to Nuku'alofa, the capital of Tonga. To our dismay, the check-in clerk initially denies us boarding. Without evidence of when we will return, our one-way ticket appears too suspicious, and the 128 kilograms of luggage exceeds the norm. I nervously and repeatedly explain our mission to the stern-looking woman and show my credit card to buy a return ticket if necessary. This eventually convinces her: she allows us to board, and we can finally rest.

Our journey takes us to Tonga, but we're not out of the woods yet. The immigration officer wants to send us straight back—no return ticket, no entry. The assumption that our contact, Mr. Hopps, had informed Immigration about us was incorrect. They've never heard of him. Exhausted and close to tears, I explain our situation repeatedly. My English is more fluent than Ivo's, so I handle the conversation. Initially, our only option seems to be buying an expensive one-year return ticket on the spot—a pretend ticket that would deplete a significant portion of our funds and be unused. Help finally arrives in the form of a sympathetic Air Pacific official who seems to empathise with us. She pulls us aside and whispers something that we struggle to understand, either because we are too tired or not accustomed to the Polynesian English accent. She discreetly hands us two return tickets, and we, dazed by jetlag, only comprehend that we should later return these to the airline office in Nuku'alofa. Soon after, the immigration officer stamps our passports with a tourist visa, and we are finally allowed to set foot on Tongan soil.

Almost there... but now, the border police closely inspect our luggage. With great curiosity, the officers spread out all our belongings on a large table. In Tongan, they engage in lengthy discussions about our solar panels, electric incubator, tripod, telescope, cameras, Walkman, and large first aid kit—not the usual items tourists usually carry. We've spent weeks carefully packing the barrels to utilise every inch of space, but now we are far too tired to repack them meticulously. Someone hands us plastic bags to stow some of our gear, and finally, 36 hours after leaving Frankfurt, we arrive in the Nuku'alofa arrival hall, loaded up like Santa himself.

Our local contact, Mr. Hopps, and his wife Susan, await us. He apologises for not resolving our immigration issues and says he lacked influence with the Immigration Department. We would have appreciated some advance notice about this problem but are far too exhausted to care now. On the drive to Mr. Hopps's house, the sights of Nuku'alofa, meaning 'City of Love,' keep us awake. We pass exotic vegetation and traditional huts made from woven coconut fronds, surrounded by free-roaming pigs, dogs, and horses.

When Mr. Hopps stops at a petrol station, we witness the preparations for a traditional two-week funeral ceremony, including the slaughter of two squealing piglets by knife. Coconuts fall from the top of a palm tree like giant hailstones, dropped by a dark-skinned Polynesian youth who has climbed the seven-metre-high palm without assistance. The people, including men, wear black skirts beneath their traditional brownish skirts made of woven pandanus leaves, called *ta'ovala*. Mr. Hopps explains that these garments are especially long during mourning. The more frayed the edges, the closer the wearer was to the deceased. What we are witnessing now are the preparations for the two-week feast following any burial.

For the first week, we stay with Mr. Hopps and his family. Later, when he needs the space, we move to a hotel. During that first week, we appreciate Mr. Hopps's and especially Susan's hospitality. Susan prepares delicious dishes from fresh fruit and root vegetables grown locally. She says she has come to appreciate the local ingredients but still misses dark German bread. Susan particularly enjoys one aspect of Tongan culture: the respect accorded to women. She explains that Tongan society is matriarchal, and women usually hold a higher social status than men. This sounds promising to me, knowing I would find it difficult to live in a society where I couldn't be as independent as at home.

While we enjoy our conversations with Susan, it is challenging to gauge our standing with Mr. Hopps. He is too busy with his zoo to discuss the details of our project, and we urgently need these discussions. He also surprises us with news that we need to undergo an AIDS test for our research permit. We thought he had already secured this permit, but apparently not. The wheels seem to turn more slowly in Tonga than in Germany, which may explain Mr. Hopps's delays. We are trying to control our impatience, which is difficult after months of preparation and the numerous obstacles we've encountered. After two weeks, Mr. Hopps still hasn't discussed the project details with us. He is always too busy, and it seems we will have to travel to Niuafo'ou on a tourist visa rather than a research visa, hoping that Mr. Hopps will handle the research permit as promised.

Apart from waiting to speak with Mr. Hopps and completing the AIDS test, we spend our two weeks in Nuku'alofa gathering more equipment and speaking with Haniteli. This empathetic young man is one of the few Tongans in the capital who has visited our distant island and can offer insights into life there, 600 km to the north. He works as a keeper in Mr. Hopps's zoo and is kind and approachable.

In brief, Haniteli describes Niuafo'ou as 'a rough island,' based on his lively experiences there. "They don't own much on that island," he says, "mainly breadfruit, some chickens, and pigs." Haniteli predicts that the locals will be very interested in us and our equipment. "Make sure they don't intrude too much on your privacy and that you only share what you want to share," he advises, also teaching us about the term pālangi. This is the Tongan word for people with white skin, and he says many locals think pālangi always give things for free. This assumption has been partly fuelled by white missionaries who visited the island in the 1800s and often gave away items to locals in exchange for attending church. "Make sure they don't think you're one of those pālangi who always give," is his last piece of advice before he hurries off to clean a birdcage.

The next day, Haniteli offers more potentially crucial advice. He emphasises that instead of giving things away for free, we need to understand the value of essential items, especially food, which we will need to obtain from locals. Money is often useless, as the only local shop has very little to sell. "Take some tins of corned beef and tobacco with you for trading; they like those things," he says, "but don't ask the locals for a price, or they'll charge you much too high!" We appreciate Haniteli's advice, but who can tell us how many sweet potatoes or breadfruit to exchange for a tin of corned beef or a pack of tobacco? We can't find that information in any travel guide.

Our next challenge is how to reach Niuafo'ou. In the 1940s and '50s, ships frequently travelled there to collect copra, the dried coconut flesh harvested from the island's thousands of palm trees. Now, with the market having ceased, ships or planes visit Niuafo'ou only sporadically, every few months. It seems we might be stuck there for extended periods. Ivo tries to highlight the positives if this happens. "Imagine sleeping in a tent under the stars for years, our tummies full of tropical fruit," he says. "Think how wonderful it will be to experience life with these Polynesian people and gain unique insights into the Malau." My initial thoughts are more along the lines of "Imagine enduring the steamy heat for months, our minds tormented by the longing for a soft bed and a shower..." But I don't finish those thoughts, as it's too unsettling to consider being stranded on the island longer than expected. It's better to follow Ivo's lead and optimistically embrace whatever comes, burying our concerns deep within.

As if to reward our optimism, Royal Tongan Airlines surprises us with good news. Until recently, they had flown to Niuafo'ou only every few months, mainly because most of the 400 inhabitants couldn't afford tickets, and tourists avoided the island. We are thrilled to learn that a new German manager has recently taken over and is keen to upgrade the service to include the outer islands in its route. Planes are now scheduled to fly to Niuafo'ou every fortnight, weather permitting.

While we appreciate this new flight option, it does not resolve our luggage problem. The airline allows only 20 kg of luggage, but ours has grown from the original 128 kg to much more. Additional items like ropes, tools, shade cloth, water canisters, kerosene, tarps, tinned food, and items for trading with locals have increased the weight. Our focus shifts to finding a vessel. We talk to numerous yacht and rusty cutter owners at the harbour, but to no avail. "We're all heading south," one of them says. "Cyclone season is approaching, and you'd better head that way too." They can't convince us to abandon our plans. We are determined to reach our island somehow.

Finally, we have some success at a local shipping company's office. One of their freight ships, the Moana, delivers goods to the outer islands, including ours, and also takes passengers—not in cabins, but on top of the metal loading hatch, with a tarp for rain and sun protection above. However, the Moana only departs in a month, and after already spending two weeks here, we're not prepared to wait that long. For now, we decide to take the plane next week and ask Mr. Hopps if he can send our equipment with the Moana when it next departs. We can only hope he will support us as initially discussed and assist with this task.

Our final preparation involves arranging accommodation on Niuafo'ou. Haniteli recommends notifying the local chief, Malohi, about our arrival. He suggests asking if we can pay Malohi to build a traditional hut made of woven coconut fronds. But how do we contact Malohi? There is one telephone on the island, but it only makes outgoing calls. Haniteli comes up with a creative solution: ask Radio Tonga to broadcast a message. A day after visiting Radio Tonga's office with our request, they broadcast an announcement in Tongan, which can be heard across all of Tonga's 171 islands. Translated, it says, "Message for Malohi on Niuafo'ou: please call Haniteli in Nuku'alofa to discuss the arrival of two pālangi." To our surprise, this radio message and one-way telephone call across 600 km of sea actually works. Haniteli proudly reports that Malohi will build our house, but we should bring plenty of tobacco in addition to paying with the local currency, Pa'anga. Haniteli says 200 Pa'anga is a fair price, so we aim for that. Ivo and I hug each other with excitement: our first house together is about to be built!

While waiting, we discuss the importance of being accepted by the locals. We want to be part of their society rather than merely visiting pālangi. Such acceptance is vital for our mental health when suggesting conservation measures for the Malau and crucial for our survival, especially since we depend on locals for food. Our first step toward better acceptance is to purchase a book titled *Intensive Course in Tongan*, and we dive into learning this new language. We will need it, as Haniteli mentions that only some younger people on Niuafo'ou speak a bit of English.

To me, who speaks Italian, Tongan sounds somewhat familiar. Each syllable ends in a vowel and contains one consonant, and many words are short. I get mixed up between Italian words like *lile, che,* or *tacchi,* and Tongan words like *lele, hake, or taki.* Some words even exist in both languages but have different meanings, such as *malo, io* and *pasta.* There are differences between these languages, though; Tongan has traps that can make you look foolish: the same written word can have different meanings depending on vowel length when pronounced. Tongans use special markings on their written vowels that change the pronunciation and thus the meaning of the word. For example, *Kaka* means parrot, whereas *Kākā* means a cheat. Similarly, adding a glottal stop before vowels can change meanings. For instance, *Uma* means kiss, while *'Uma* means shoulder. It might be interesting to ask for a shoulder on the cheek instead of a kiss on the cheek. We accept that we may often look foolish, but we are having great fun learning together and testing each other's understanding. For example, I cause some laughter when I forget the phrase *pongipongi 'apongipongi te u 'alu ai ki ha paati*—Tomorrow morning, I will go to a party.

3

Suddenly on the Moana

Flexibility seems to be the key to survival in Tonga, and ours is tested when, in early September, we casually call the office of the Moana vessel the day before our booked flight to Niuafo'ou. "Just calling to confirm your departure date in a month so we can arrange for the transport of our luggage," I say, unaware that this call will disrupt our plans. "No, not in a month," the friendly lady replies nonchalantly. "We are now leaving at 9 pm tonight, and all luggage needs to be on board by 4 pm." My request to repeat this information confirms the urgency. It's either tonight or no transport for many months, especially with the cyclone season approaching.

There's no question: we will now travel on this vessel too. We can ensure our luggage gets to the island, avoid bothering Mr. Hopps, and save the money for the plane trip. Our new plan gives us two hours to pack and label all our equipment and settle the hotel bill. What a rush! "I was looking forward to one more night in a real bed," I regretfully say to Ivo. He, who cares less about comfort than I do, shrugs it off. "You'll sleep under the stars on the Pacific Ocean soon," he replies. Sweaty and exhausted, we barely make it to the boat by 4 pm, only thanks to Susan Hopps, who kindly drives us and all our luggage to the harbour.

While Ivo ensures that our belongings don't 'accidentally' get lost and actually reach the ship's loading area, I return the plane tickets and rush through the shops to gather food for the three-day trip to Niuafo'ou. I pack these extras into one of those cheap, large stripy zipper bag that locals carry everywhere. With our initial plan, we had limited our luggage to essentials to avoid burdening Mr. Hopps, but now I can add a few luxuries: a bottle of red wine and two small novels from the 'Friendly Island Bookshop.' When I tell Ivo later, he is pleased with my purchases but has one complaint: "Why didn't you get any biscuits and chocolate?" Sorry, Ivo, it didn't occur to me, and I forgot how much of a sweet tooth you have. Let's hope we can find some sugary treats in the coming months.

Before departure, we also rush to Radio Tonga. "Can you please broadcast a message to Malohi on Niuafo'ou that the two pālangis will now arrive on the Moana in three days?" The lady in the office agrees with a nod, treating the request as routine. No need to mention our names, as we will likely be the only pālangis travelling to that distant island. Despite the announcement being broadcast across Tonga's 171 islands, the message is likely to be overlooked by most people among personal updates about marriages and other local news.

Once aboard the Moana, three large, chatty families are travelling with us on the rusted vessel, totalling about 40 people. Every group claims their space on the metal hatch of the loading deck with a wall of stripy zipper bags, melons, pots, cardboard boxes, handwoven mats, baskets with chickens, and live pigs in hessian bags. We have fewer items—small backpacks, three solar panels, and two stripy bags—but are glad to have packed our blow up camping mats in our hand luggage for some comfort. Our sleeping bags are tucked away in our remaining luggage in the main hold, which we can't access. In all the rush, it didn't occur to us to leave them out.

Before we set off, an Englishman on the pier informs us that the rusty Moana was built over 40 years ago for river transport in China, not for the high seas we're about to navigate. He mentions that a similar ship disappeared en route to Niuafo'ou some years ago, with all passengers lost. It's too late to change our plans now, so we choose to ignore this unsettling detail. Instead, we enjoy the first few hours of the trip, especially the music from a group of young men playing various string instruments like ukuleles. Some well-built Tongan women sing along, projecting their voices far and wide. They clear some luggage from the deck to create a small dance floor where children and adults happily dance at sea. By midnight, everyone falls asleep on their rolled-out mats.

On the first night and day, people don't interact much with us, leaving us alone in our claimed space at the edge of the metal hatch. This changes almost immediately after we depart Vava'u, the island group halfway between Nuku'alofa and Niuafo'ou. Our fellow travellers are astonished that we two pālangis are not disembarking at this favourite tourist spot but are travelling on to Niuafo'ou. They seem to have missed the radio message. Unfortunately, our Tongan isn't fluent enough for lengthy conversations, so we can only exchange smiles. We are relieved to find one older man named Laione who speaks some English. His face lights up when he learns we will be living on Niuafo'ou to study the Malau. Soon, everyone on the ship knows. The kind people around us share coconuts, roast chicken, and taro. Many move closer to sit with us and check us out. While we eat with our hands, the ship's cook serves us hot tea and crackers, which makes us feel a bit embarrassed but highlights that we are indeed the only pālangi and are treated differently.

Laione is particularly excited because eleven years ago, he hosted David Todd, the last researcher who studied the Malau. Demonstrating unique facial expressions, Laione lies on the floor, mimicking Todd crawling through the bush with binoculars glued to his eyes. The Tongans on deck are highly amused by Laione's storytelling and acting. We wonder if, in the future, we too will become the subject of such entertaining tales. The laughter of our fellow passengers is a welcome distraction from the rough conditions of a ship not designed for passenger comfort—windy, cold, with only one outhouse toilet without running water, occasionally flushed with water from buckets.

The next day, we lie on our mats under the tarp, listening to the relentless buffeting of waves and swaying with the ship's movement, which groans and creaks as it pushes through the Pacific Ocean. Occasionally, we sit up to warm our frozen bodies or rearrange our bags as a makeshift windbreak for a game of chess on our small travel set. Mostly, we lie there, slightly seasick and semi-dormant. Our fellow travellers have also become quiet, stretched out on woven pandanus mats. Laione chats with us occasionally, noting that people on the main island, Tongatapu, regard Niuafo'ou as a traditional island. "This is both good and bad," he says. "Good because it means we remember the old ways and keep our traditions; bad because they think we are backward." It reminds me of my homeland, Austria, where city dwellers often looked down on those from small mountain villages as naïve. I struggled with this perception when I was the first girl from my village to attend high school in the main town.

After the third night on deck, a group of young men wake us at 5 am with a traditional song that stirs our emotions. The song is a continuous 'story,' with each person singing a different part. The men sing in high falsetto, while the women join in with their deep, sad voices. Though we don't understand the storyline, it sends shivers of emotion and joy down our spines. "A song about ancestors," Laione explains. "Ancestors are very important to Tongan people. An old song," he adds. "Learned from parents and grandparents." His explanation aligns with our travel guide, which notes that ancestry plays a significant role in Tongan identity and is preserved through oral traditions.

It's also fascinating to think we are among the first people on this globe to welcome each new day. Our vessel travels just west of the International Date Line, so in the morning, we are the first to greet a new day, while people a few kilometres to the east are still in the previous day. We've heard that the Vava'u group in Tonga sees an influx of date-hopping tourists on New Year's Eve, people who want to celebrate New Year's twice—once on this side of the Date Line and again the next day, on islands further east.

4

Jumping Ashore

Three weeks after leaving Frankfurt, we arrive at Niuafo'ou on the morning of the third day of our boat trip. There is one more hurdle left to overcome: getting from the ship to the land. The lava flows from past eruptions of the local volcano have left a rugged, dangerous shoreline that would tear apart the hull of our boat. Instead, a rock platform that protrudes into the sea serves as a landing place. Calling it a jetty would be a bit of an exaggeration. Geologically, this only landing place on the island, called Futu, is the end of a lava flow that originated from a volcanic eruption many years ago. Smaller boats are needed to take people to this platform, and quite often, they must wait for several days before they can land because the sea is too rough. We sigh with relief that the sea is relatively calm and cooperative today, but we still have to practice our patience. Before the captain has even dropped the anchor, three young men from Niuafo'ou arrive in their small, about 7-metre-long tinny with an outboard engine. They are barefoot and bearded, wearing tattered singlets and shorts, and their dark skin above and around the knees is covered in tattoos. Their first demand is for cigarette paper and tobacco. They have long since run out and are desperate for a smoke, as the island hasn't seen a supply ship for months.

Disembarkation only begins once the men have slowly rolled their cigarettes and finished their smoke. One of the men turns to us. "*10 Pa'anga to go land,*" he demands with a stern look. He doesn't ask any of the Tongans to pay for this transport ashore, but it is clear they expect white people to have money. The last time they collected this payment must have been quite some years ago. We have no choice but to pay. At least our fare includes a helping hand to step from the rusty ladder into the rickety boat, a snug seat among numerous people who cram into the boat like sardines, and some powerful arms to pull us from the boat onto the rock platform at the right moment. The right moment is not to be missed and is extremely short, determined by when the crest of a wave lifts the boat high enough for people to jump ashore quickly. We cling to our three solar panels during this transfer and are relieved that these, and our remaining hand luggage, somehow make it ashore unharmed.

Left to ourselves on the platform, we walk to an open area behind the landing site surrounded by mango trees and small shade shelters made of woven mats. This 'harbour' area in the western part of the island lies five or more kilometres from the villages in the northern and northeastern regions. Still, the distance has not deterred the many locals who have gathered to welcome the boat, especially the supplies. Our arrival, broadcast on Radio Tonga, may have attracted more onlookers, and many people are staring at us. We are, after all, the first pālangis who have visited this island in a while, and it seems like we are the only ones on the whole island now. People are reserved and keep their distance but offer a subtle smile whenever our eyes meet.

An older man approaches us and shakes our hands. "Malohi?" we ask, and he nods. This must be our host. He greets us with a friendly but reserved smile and doesn't speak any English. "*Talitali fiefia*"—"welcome"—he says, and all we can do is smile back and say hi in Tongan—"*Malo e lelei.*" Luckily, a young man standing next to him introduces himself as his son, and he understands English well enough to comprehend that all our luggage needs to come ashore. So we ask him to look for fifteen items labelled with 'Malau,' and he returns to the ship to diligently search for them in the vast hold of the boat.

While people can jump ashore, luggage cannot. Strong folk on the rock platform have to catch it after the people in the tinny throw the bags and boxes to them. Again, this must happen at the right moment when the waves help out, and it is no easy feat when the luggage is heavy, like our wooden trunks. Somehow, through a fantastic team effort by strong young men, all our belongings are brought ashore and loaded onto the trailer of Malohi's tractor.

Three tractors, including Malohi's, are the only powered vehicles on the island and are considered the luxury mode of transportation. Otherwise, people walk or ride on horseback. Having slept little on the ship, we are dead tired and more than glad to commute on the trailer. Malohi takes the only route connecting the landing site with all eight villages and a grass strip that calls itself an airport. The island road consists of two muddy tracks full of puddles, separated by a middle strip where the lush vegetation is slightly lower than along the edge of the tracks. Sitting on our barrels and being shaken each time we hit a pothole, we enjoy the tropical green and warm air around us. My body is still swaying from the long trip on the Moana.

The island is home to about 400 people, and the first village we enter is Esia, one of the largest settlements on the island. Here, a freshly thatched palm-frond hut awaits us, next to Malohi's cooking house. Our home looks rather romantic, like a green hideaway. Apart from a frame made of wooden logs and a wooden door, every other part consists of mats. Each mat consists of half a coconut palm frond, of which the leaflets are interwoven to form a mat about one metre long. The whole house is covered in these mats, tied to the wooden frame in an overlapping fashion. A narrow area at the side is left open as a window for airflow. The floor measures 18 square metres and is layered with several of these mats. It is decorated with a beautifully embellished mat woven from the leaves of the pandanus trees, which are also called screwpines and are abundant on this island. We admire this present from the local ladies and are thrilled to have finally arrived.

5

Settling in and a Church Service

On our arrival, Malohi's large family watches us from a distance, and we try to convey our joy about the new hut with smiles and gestures. A little later, we chat with his teenage daughter Laveni, who speaks a few words of English. "Beautiful hut and nice island," I say. "Thank you for the beautiful mat." She proudly smiles from one ear to the other. Then, with her help, we hand over tobacco and payment for the house and, in return, are given a welcome feast. Malohi's family has roasted a whole piglet just for us, and they deliver the entire animal to our hut, served on banana leaves, with manioc on the side. The meat is tender and melts in our mouths, but it's far too much. We hope not to offend our hosts by returning the piglet half-eaten and with the fatty outer blubber and head not touched. Next, two children deliver some young coconuts to drink, but they are somewhat scared of us. It appears they have never seen a white person before. They run over to our house, throw the coconuts through the door, and are gone before we can even say *malo*—thank you—to them.

Esia consists of a loose assembly of houses built from either woven mats, corrugated iron, or lava stone. The few lava stone houses are more substantial structures, held together with concrete. In contrast to the thatched palm-frond huts, they have genuine windows and doors and a corrugated iron roof. Like the other huts, though, they only have one room. Our place is surrounded by an outhouse toilet made of corrugated iron, our washroom, and the cooking hut. The open-air 'washroom' consists of a tiny uncovered area separated by a wall of woven mats that reaches up to our neck and contains one board to place a bowl on. Of course, there is no running water; it needs to be fetched from a tank nearby.

The house next door is a solid lava stone building and seems to be inhabited by a large group of young men, all unmarried. We have read that in Tonga, young men are separated from their families as soon as they have reached puberty. It is *tapu*—taboo—for such teenagers to be in the same room as their sister or girl cousins alone, and our family seems to have solved this problem by housing all the bachelors in one house. One of the teens walks past, sending us a big smile while carrying a large round stone on his shoulder. He gestures to us that this is the pillow he will use when slumbering on the floor. We are so tired that even a concrete floor with a stone pillow would be heaven right now.

Malohi's cooking house is a palm-frond hut with a covered roof like ours, but its sides are open. Inside, the women have just cooked our pig in the traditional earth oven called *umu*. It consists of a one-metre-deep hole in the ground in which the ladies make a fire to heat some lava stones. Once the rocks are hot enough, the food is wrapped up in banana leaves, placed on the stones, and then covered with soil. After some hours, the oven is uncovered, and the food emerges cooked.

We don't have much time to scan our surroundings as we are busy staying awake. It would be too easy to give in to our sleepiness, which has increased threefold after eating half a pig. It is Sunday, after all, and this is when you go to church. *Lotu*—church—becomes the first word of Tongan we learn from Malohi when he comes to fetch us. "*Lotu?*" he first says gently, but when we gesture that we don't understand, this becomes "*Lotu!*" accompanied by a stern look and pointing towards the church. So off he walks; there is no question whether we will follow or not. So off we walk too, direction Catholic church, with Malohi's large family group of about seventeen people—adults, children of all ages, and a baby. We have no idea who belongs to whom as so far, we have only met one son and his daughter Laveni.

We are still wearing our clothes from the ferry. There was no time to get changed or freshen up, so we now feel sticky and underdressed among the churchgoers. We are glad to at least wear long sleeves and pants, as everyone wears modest long clothes, clearly the best ones they own. The men all wear spotless white western-style shirts on top, and on the bottom, the traditional two layers of wraparound skirts: a white cloth skirt underneath a shorter woven skirt tied around the waist with a string. These *ta'ovalas*—woven skirts—are crafted from the leaves of the pandanus tree and are a work of art, often decorated with coloured wool around the bottom edge. The women wear a very colourful dress underneath their *ta'ovalas*, which are longer than those of the men and more decorated. The young girls are spruced up in doll-like dresses, the boys in shirts and shorts, and all walk barefoot. Thongs don't seem decent enough for church, even though the people seem to wear them at all other times.

In church, I only wished I had one of those homemade woven fans that all the other women carry with them to fan themselves some fresh air. It is so sticky and hot, and the only thing that keeps me awake during the three-hour service in Tongan is the crying of the babies and the volume of the singing. Men and women sit separated on opposite sides of the church, and I don't even dare send a glance to Ivo as everyone seems to be watching me. The volume of the ladies' singing is unlike anything I have ever heard before, and soon, my eardrums start ringing.

Back at our hut, we walk like in a trance while fetching water, cleaning ourselves up over a bowl, and somehow pushing aside our equipment so that we have room to sleep on the floor. The long voyage on the Moana, the pig feast, humidity, heat, and church service have left us too tired to blow up our camping mattresses or rummage for our sheets and mosquito nets that are hidden somewhere in our bags. So instead, we fall into an exhausted daytime sleep curled up on the decorative floor mat. Our dreams mingle with the many noises around us—buzzing mosquitos, people laughing and chatting next door, babies crying, and the varying noises uttered by the pigs, goats, dogs, and roosters that roam around freely in the village.

6

A First Taste of Village Life—and Muttonbirds

Our daily interactions with Chief Malohi mainly consist of smiles and gestures during the next week, though we are slowly picking up some more Tongan. Food-related words are the most important ones. "*Fiekaia?*"—"hungry?"—Malohi asks when bringing a meal, followed by his appreciative smile when we reply "*io*"—"yes"—while rubbing our bellies. "*Lelei 'aupito!*"—"very good!"—is also an essential phrase we need to utter when returning the plates. What we didn't know, though, is that the Tongan we have learnt from our book is not spoken the same way up here. The language of Niuafo'ou is a unique mixture of Tongan, Samoan, and the languages of nearby Wallis and Futuna. After all, Niuafo'ou is closer to these other islands than the remaining Tongan archipelago.

Our vocabulary is not sufficient to discuss catering, as we want to agree with Malohi's family on a set amount of payment in return for regular weekly meals. We need the help of a local translator who speaks some English. Malohi recruits Salesi, the man who serves as both post and bank officer for the island. This chap seems reputable and agrees to translate, and soon the meal deal with Malohi is done. Salesi then asks us for a favour in return: "When you next order some goods from the main island, could you also include two tins of yeast so that I can bake some bread?" We agree, thinking what a good cause it would be to help him bake some bread. What we don't know is that this could get us in serious trouble with the law.

The law on Niuafo'ou is represented by the one and only local police officer, Kailao. Soon after our translator has left, Kailao visits in official police uniform—a white shirt with a police star on it, a dark skirt, and a police hat. He has a stern look on his face because he is following up on some serious news that has spread like wildfire: the pālangis have brought lots of alcohol to the island. What else would they carry in heavy, sturdy wooden chests like ours? Alcohol is forbidden on Niuafo'ou, as it has caused mayhem in the past. Kailao asks us to show him our trunks and valuables. He becomes less stern after we have complied and shown him everything, except the one bottle of wine hidden away in the corner of our hut. Then, he promises to watch over our belongings whenever we are in the field to study the birds. We appreciate this offer as we know from Haniteli that people share everything they have with their family and friends in Tongan culture, and the locals will expect that of us too.

Looking after our belongings is a new job that Kailao now adds to his official duties as a police officer. These jobs usually consist of hoisting the Tongan flag in the mornings, finding stolen pigs or barbed wire, and arresting men who have consumed homebrew alcohol. He detains people in the only cell inside the police station and tells us the cell has no bars or locked doors. It is just a regular room—inmates here don't escape because where could they go on an island isolated by several hundred kilometres of ocean?

Kailao's English is quite fluent, and from now on, he stops by every day. Officially, he needs to check on our belongings; unofficially, he admits that he enjoys chatting with us and learning about our culture. We feel the same when talking to him. He also informs us that the post, aka bank manager, would not use the yeast he ordered from us for bread baking but for making homebrew alcohol that is illegal on the island. Giving yeast to the locals is also against the law. To avoid sitting in Kailao's jail, we had better not fulfil our promise to Salesi, the apparently not-so-reputable post and bank manager.

Kailao proudly tells us that his name means 'war dance', but he has no idea why his parents chose this name. On Tongatapu, we learned that Tongans often name their babies after big events, famous people, flowers, or biblical names. One man we met there was called Keneti and was named after the US president J.F. Kennedy because one of his relatives was also a politician in Tonga. Recent innovations can also spark exciting names. For example, we had the pleasure of meeting Olivetti and Panasonic, two men named after certain products from these companies that had finally reached Tongan shelves. Often, the names are based on an English word spelt the Tongan way. For example, men might be called Laione for lion, Aisi for ice, Fokisi for fox, or Pasilo for Basil, whereas women might carry names such as Safaia for sapphire, Emeni for amen, Musica for music, or Silika for silk.

On our fifth day, Kailao and Lakepi, Malohi's adult son, offer us the chance to join them on a nightly trip that provides a unique cultural insight. After dark, the four of us and a pack of dogs venture through large uninhabited, barren lava fields to the rocky western shore. The men are about to practise an old custom not known from many other Pacific islands: hunting Wedge-tailed shearwaters (*Puffinus pacificus*), a type of muttonbird, from the air. These seabirds are champions at racking up frequent-flyer miles. They fly thousands of kilometres over the open sea to find food but come close to islands like Niuafo'ou after dark. Here they circle swiftly not too far from shore, and this is what our two guides rely on. Soon after sunset, they stand on the outermost tip of a rock that protrudes out from the shore, armed with a long, flexible wooden stick. They have lit a fire nearby, on a small grassy patch that will become our refuge for the night. The lava fields around us are a stark reminder of the last volcanic eruption, and we push aside any thoughts about the predictions that this island volcano could erupt again. Instead, we watch as the two men loudly utter eerie calls that sound like wolves howling and could have come straight out of a haunted house. After 10 minutes, the first shearwaters are attracted by these calls and circle overhead. Then, at the right moment and with exceptional skill, the men use their long poles to hit the fast-flying birds in the air so that their wings become damaged, and they tumble to the ground. There, the waiting dogs immediately catch the poor things and deliver them to the men. The mongrels accumulate about twenty of the unfortunate fluffballs before midnight.

While the two men seem to appreciate our participation, we have to bite our tongues about the birds' cruel treatment. Our empathy would be unwelcome when they are hunting for their dinner. The mutton birds are coarsely plucked, mainly alive, and then thrown straight into the fire. Our protest against animal cruelty would not change this tradition and would only yield laughter, but we do not consume much of the oily-tasting birds. Lakepi and Kailao seem to convey that they admire us for sleeping on the little grassy patch out in the open all night, joining them in fishing, and eating the fish and birds that look rather unappetising when burnt black from the fire.

Our fishing skills need improving, though. The men don't use rods, only a 100-metre-long fishing line which they place down on the rock in front of them, arranged in a loose loop. They attach a piece of crab to the hook and then throw the line far out into the sea, like a lasso swung by a cowboy. It looks so easy, but when we try with only a 20-metre-long line, it gets caught on the rocks until we end up with one big knot instead of a fish in our hands.

Biting our tongues about animal cruelty has already been hard before. We have seen piglets stored in hessian bags on the ship and left to lie in the burning sun for hours. In the village, dogs are beaten and kicked, and horses have ribs sticking out like skeletons because they only get fed palm fronds. The mongrels that run around in packs all over the island are flea-infested and love to bark. All they get provided with are the occasional scrap and a bit of copra, the 'flesh' of ripened coconuts. When meat for human consumption is rare, these dogs occasionally end up in the earth oven. The only proper pet dog on the island, well-fed and groomed, is owned by a nun who is originally from Tongatapu. When we recently met after church, she confessed that she cherishes her pup like the apple of her eye, and she is worried that it too may end up as someone's dinner one day.

We have already noticed that the pigs in the village are fed more than the dogs, mainly copra. Their meat is an integral part of local feasts, and coconut flesh tends to increase the fat content of the meat—the fatter, the higher the value. We read that during feasts, people of esteem are served the skin and thick fat blubber underneath first before others get their share. Pigs in Tonga are not the pink pigs we know from Europe but a longhaired breed that comes in all kinds of amusing rusty brown to black colours and patterns. When the pigs are not busy poking their noses into pots left cooking on the fire, they love digging things up with their snouts. The soft soil around our freshly built hut seems to be their favourite spot, especially near the foundations. Thus, we live with almost constant background noise from hordes of grunting pigs, all day and most of the night. Pigs don't seem to sleep much. This noise is regularly interspersed with even louder grunting when pigs get chased by a pack of dogs, also day and night. Dogs don't seem to sleep much either.

For some strange reason, people here don't keep their pigs in pens. This habit saves them from making fences but ignores the fact that they have to find even more barriers to surround their plantations, which are much bigger than a pig corral would be. Such fences are hard to come by, and thus entire crops often get destroyed by hordes of pigs devouring them instead. It also explains Kailao's story that stealing fences is one of the top crimes he regularly has to solve.

7

Monster Centipedes

While we explore the island in the daytime during the next few weeks, our little hut mainly serves as a refuge after dark. Not on Sundays, though, as these are days of rest and worship. Under Tongan law, people are not allowed to conduct business or work on Sundays, and on the mainland, public transport is also not available on that day. At least we don't have to worry about public transport here.

After Sunday church, we enjoy each other's company in our hut, where we find lots to giggle and joke about. For example, we have to tell people that we are married, as in Tonga, it is highly inappropriate for a man and woman to live together before they have tied the knot. There is no need to tell our hosts that we have only known each other for seven months and that we would still like to pass this 'island test' together before even thinking about such an alliance. In our culture, this is fine, but not in theirs. So far, so good. We get on well most of the time, except when we quarrel about how to best store our stuff in the hut. Somehow, we seem to be searching for something constantly. Our home is not exactly spacious, but on our third Sunday in Esia, we are considerably improving its interior and exterior design.

The exterior design receives a boost when we attach some of our shade cloth to the open side 'windows'. This new window covering has several important functions. First, it stops the kids from constantly reaching in. The youngsters have lost all their fear of us, and we like to entertain them by showing some of our things or letting them draw something with our pens and paper. Their little fingers frequently come poking through the window opening, and so far, we have always had to make sure nothing of value was placed within reach. Second, the shade cloth is a bit of a visual barrier, so people can't look in as much as before, and it thus gives us some privacy for the occasional hug or two. Tongans regard it as highly inappropriate to display any affection between members of the opposite gender in public. Even parents don't usually show affection towards their children when others are around.

Our shade cloth's most crucial function is to reduce somewhat the number of mosquitoes entering. Unfortunately, the bloodsucking pests still find holes to enter, and we continue to sleep under mosquito nets and use repellent all day. I have laughed at Ivo at home for packing his thick woollen socks for a trip to the tropics, but now I am envious, as they prevent him from getting stung on the feet. Apart from these socks, Ivo has also brought lots of tea bags, as he believes that drinking hot tea in a sweltering climate helps you sweat more and adapt better to the heat. He might be correct, but it's too hot for me. I only manage to gulp down litres of the brackish-tasting water from the tank in an attempt to cool down my body temperature. One of the ladies from Malohi's clan kindly gave me one of those home-woven fans, which gets used a lot on this hot Sunday at home.

We also install our solar panels on the roof. Strictly speaking, this means working on a Sunday, but we hope nobody minds as long as we don't ask others to work. The panels provide us with much-needed light during the 12-hour-long tropical nights, even though we feel a bit guilty that our home is the only one in the village with electricity. Some locals have battery-powered lights, but they mostly only use kerosene lights or sleep soon after dark. Some years back, missionaries installed solar panels on the church nearby, but, as is often the case, such technology brought in by white people has not been maintained and broke down soon after.

Our interior design receives a boost when we install a pulley system that lets us hoist up our sleeping bags and mats to use the precious floor space for sitting during the day. The barrels and wooden trunks serve as welcome furniture to sit, eat, and write on, as we are not as good as the locals at sitting on the floor all day. Sunday is an excellent time to write long letters to my parents in which I detail our life on the island. Hopefully, a ship or plane will come to bring them closer to their destination one day. While I write, Ivo creates the first report for the Professor. We are also busy washing our sweat-drenched clothes and looking after our technical equipment, such as the camera, tape recorder, and microphone. These things quickly grow fungus in such humidity, so we store them in a barrel with silica gel beads, which reduces the air's moisture content. Every day, we heat the beads over our fuel stove, which releases the moisture and lets us reuse them again.

Our quiet Sunday is interrupted by the appearance of an enormous centipede that crawls leisurely along our floor. At home, these critters are small, but here in the tropics, large centipedes of the genus Scolopendra can reach a size of up to 30 cm, are carnivorous, and rather venomous. Ours is 'only' 12 cm long, but only yesterday, Kailao told us stories of how these roommates regularly bite people in their sleep and cause a lot of pain and nasty swellings that last for days. After all, it makes sense—if you are a centipede and want to eat the meat of animals bigger than you, you inject poison into them first. There is no need to wait for that, so we gently guide him outside, hoping that he will never find his way back.

Luckily, we found the centipede before it did find us, as such a bite would probably force us to take up the only bed in the local 'hospital'. As it turns out, we are not the only ones with electricity in the village—the hospital does have one light bulb operated by a generator for some hours of the day. Unfortunately, this seems to be the only bit of trustworthy technology in that hospital, as our sneak peeks through the window don't reveal much else than a bed. We are also unsure how much we would rely on the local 'medical officer' should we become sick. Kailao tells us that seriously ill people get picked up by helicopter and transported the 400 km to Vava'u. That is, if a chopper is available at that time. Let's hope that we will never need such a service and that our well-equipped first aid kit will do the job.

Also on our to-do list for today is improving our relationship with Salesi, the post and bank manager. Now that we haven't ordered the yeast as discussed initially, he seems rather upset. A plane has landed recently, and we have been waiting for mail but didn't receive any. Only a week later did Salesi hand over our letters to us. So today, we give him some corned beef as a thank you, even though mail delivery is supposed to be his job. Hopefully, this gift will make up for the missing home-brew ingredient and ensure a more prompt mail service next time.

8

Finding the Malau

At the end of September, after three weeks in Esia, we feel as though we have settled in and established some essential bonds with the locals. It is high time to venture into the inner parts of the caldera, where the Malau bird is supposed to occur, somewhere in the dense jungle around the crater lake. Such an expedition requires walking along the island road, climbing the 200 m-high crater rim, and then descending the steep paths to the lake. We borrow one of Malohi's horses for the one-hour trip, so we don't have to carry all our equipment. This plan requires one of us to sit on the horse and hold onto our backpack barrel. Never mind that Ivo has never been on a horse before. It is worth the sight, seeing him clumsily clinging to the mare's neck with one arm and our barrel with the other, much to our and all the villagers' amusement as they see us passing by. The thin horse comes more or less nude, with only an old hessian bag on its back and a rope tied around its snout. Its backbones stick out and rub uncomfortably against our sitting bones, so we welcome the times when we can swap sitting with walking.

The views from the crater rim distract us in our search for the Malau. We are awestruck and can't get enough of the fantastic vistas down to the shimmering lake with its islets and the different shades of green. On one side, a small peninsula that protrudes into the lake is dark green from thousands of Ironbark trees, also known as Casuarina trees. On the other side, lighter green is reflected off the numerous coconut palms and rainforest trees along the crater walls. The crater lake is our favourite destination, and if we could, we would spend all day fooling around in the refreshing water. A swim is such a luxury without showers in the village. It also helps relieve the itch from the many mosquito bites that torment us and washes off the constant sweat we accumulate in this humid climate. Local decency forbids us, especially me as a woman, from swimming uncovered, so I do it with all my clothes. Women in Tonga are always expected to wear clothes that cover most parts of their bodies. I read somewhere that even the beauty contest for Miss Tonga excludes the programme where the young ladies usually parade in swimsuits. At the lake, our horse gets a good splash, too, and seems to enjoy this unknown treat just as much as we do. It also gulps down the juicy grasses nearby.

We have yet to lay eyes on the Malau. The birds are elusive, and all we have in hand is a map in which our predecessor David Todd marked some of their egg-laying grounds along the edge of the crater lake. Our searches in those areas bear no fruit until the next day when three local men come swimming our way. They carry a bundle made of leaves, from which they dig out a present for us: one egg of the Malau. We politely refuse, telling them that we are here to protect the birds, not to eat their eggs. Our response might offend them and become story material for village conversations, but we need to make our position clear from the start.

At least we now know the direction the men have come from, and after swimming to the hidden clearing among the dense jungle, our waterproof barrels in tow, we find the first egg-laying ground of the Malau. An assembly of burrows is dug into the loose volcanic sand, where the earth's temperature increases with depth. The birds have used these sites for many generations. We know how other closely related species that live on volcanic islands like Palau lay their eggs, and assume this is the same for the Malau. First, they dig a deep tunnel into the burrow, measure the temperature with a sensor in their palate, and then deposit one egg if it is warm enough before scratching together soil to fill the hole again. They repeat this process a few days later when the next egg is ready to be buried. Here on this island, the locals seem to know most of these laying sites and visit them to dig out the eggs for their consumption. But for us, many questions remain to be answered about the breeding conditions, intervals between eggs, pair bonding of the bird, the number of birds still present, and many others. But of course, to answer those, we first need to find all the other hidden egg-laying grounds. Today's experience has shown us that without help, we are unlikely to discover them all.

First, we ask Laione for help, the friendly man who entertained us with his story about David Todd on the Moana. He lives in a village down the road, is delighted to see us, and immediately offers help. First, we have a long chat, during which he admits that he hopes to leave the island one day to give his six children a better education. He says that the one high school on the island is obligatory up to the age of 17, but the English lessons are somewhat rudimentary. We spend the whole next day searching for egg-laying grounds with Laione but only find one. Instead, he tells us lots of local names of plants and animals, which we also collect, and together we find many other stories to laugh about. One of these is the story of "big fat and small fat". In Tonga, being "big fat" is a status symbol and much desired. So Laione jokes with us, in a non-derogatory way, that we are both not big fat enough, only small fat, and that we need to eat more to grow horizontally.

Upon our return to Esia, we find that Malohi is angry with us because, to his dismay, we have used Laione as our guide and not his son, Lakepi, who is known as the local expert in digging up Malau eggs. It looks like we have no choice but to pay Lakepi to take us to those egg-laying grounds, and we dutifully do so over the next three days. With Lakepi, we find all the egg-laying grounds, but unfortunately, our guide uses these trips to collect eggs for his family. It seems a hopeless venture to tell Lakepi to stop doing that while we are here. He speaks no English, and even if he did, he would not view it favourably if we tried to prevent him from doing what he has always done. Theoretically, the Malau are protected by Tongan law, but most people here disregard this. We manage to return some eggs to the burrows unharmed, but Lakepi does take some despite our attempts to stop him. So unfortunately for the Malau, our paid trip is also a welcome opportunity to supplement Lakepi's dinner menu.

At one egg-laying site, he lies with his upper body and head deep in a burrow, furiously digging up the sand. He has already found twelve eggs in this same burrow. Suddenly we hear him call out, "*oih.*" Instead of an egg, he has found a freshly hatched chick at 1.3 m depth, and he retreats from the burrow to deliver the squirming feathered bundle into my hands. I am happy that this petite chick avoided the fate of being eaten by hatching just before Lakepi uncovered its earthly nest. Had it still been in the egg, it would have been collected and consumed like the others—according to Kailao, some eggs are softer after cooking, and some have a bit of crunch to them, depending on what stage of development the chicks are in.

I keep the cute youngster warm before releasing him into the forest, where he scuttles away into the understorey. We have saved him a bit of work, as usually he would have had to dig himself out from 1.3 m depth, through layers of sand, twigs, and pebbles, all by himself. I knew from the books that this is how megapode chicks start their life, but only now do I believe it, and I am deeply fascinated. It is too hard to grasp if you haven't seen it, as no other bird starts its life so deep down in the soil and without any parental care.

While our primary motivation for this expedition is the conservation of the Malau, we also have vague hopes that we might get enough data on the birds to write a Master's thesis. We are both not fixed on this, as the focus is on data that serves the conservation purpose, but if it did materialise, it would help us progress in our studies. This project swallows two years of our degree, and it would help if we could make up for this by working towards a Master's thesis. While the freshly hatched Malau rests in my hands, I realise that my fascination with these chicks could be a good seed for making the egg and chick development topics for my thesis. That is, if I can get enough observations on these youngsters. Ivo has not yet decided on a potential topic. For now, while Lakepi digs, we at least take some basic measurements of the egg-laying burrows and temperatures inside them. We plan to come back later to continue our studies of the laying grounds without damaging the eggs. Hopefully, we will also lay eyes on some adults who visit the burrows.

The logistics of our trips with Lakepi differ considerably for him and us. He carries only his machete, tobacco, a bit of fishing line with a hook, and a scarf around his head. We take a waterproof barrel with technical equipment, notebooks, spare clothes, first aid, water, and corned beef. Swimming is required to reach most of the Malau's laying grounds. I admire how Lakepi just uses his scarf to tie his tobacco to his head, cuts off a pole from a beach hibiscus tree, walks into the lake with all his clothes on, and uses the pole as a float for himself and the machete while kicking his way through the lake. His facial expressions clearly show how amused he is by our way of doing things; for example, we take four times as long to pack and unpack our equipment into and out of the barrel before the return swim. We offer to add his tobacco to the waterproof luggage, but he declines with an amused smile.

He also laughs in a slightly condescending way when we take all our measurements while he digs up the Malau eggs, as he can't see the purpose of this. Often, he hands us some young coconuts and then demonstrates how to open a nut with just three hits of the machete. This action usually results in a nice round hole just big enough to drink the refreshing coconut water from. However, our hits create nothing but a mess of the coconut and another big smile on Lakepi's face. Lakepi talks a lot to us in Tongan, and when we don't understand, he grins from ear to ear. We feel a bit put off by his demeanour, but it appears that it is quite normal here to make fun of someone in their presence. Maybe it's a bonding thing, and we should be proud that Lakepi treats us this way?

While our guide provides the drinks, quickly retrieved from some coconut palms, we provide a meal that he can't easily get: corned beef. We have brought along a few tins based on Haniteli's advice in Nuku'alofa, but we have not understood what a much-sought-after delicacy this is for the locals. Lakepi devours it, but when we try to ingest the salty bits of beef, we have to close our eyes and not think, as they contain more fat and blood vessels than actual meat. In short, we find it disgusting. Lakepi thanks us for his treat by catching and cooking some Tilapia fish in return. These small fish occur in high numbers in the crater lake, and Lakepi pulls out one after the other with his fishing line and a worm attached to the hook.

While we appreciate his friendly offer, cooked on a small fire, we have trouble eating the fish. The bony lunch is burnt black outside and still partly raw inside. Also, the fish still contain the gall bladder, which gives them a bitter taste. All conversations cease while Lakepi sucks the eyeballs and crunches the less-formidable bones. Ivo only pretends to nibble on this snack and gulps down some corned beef with disgust, whereas I am hungry enough to eat the fish, eyeballs excluded. I still find it a better option than corned beef, especially as I had been a vegetarian up until a few weeks ago. At home, Ivo realistically told me that I would have to eat whatever we could get on this trip, and I think he is right.

9

Culinary Insights

One particular piglet steals my heart among the many pigs roaming around the village. We call it 'Schweinchen', even though we know that this secret pet of ours might not have the longest life. It is adorable, light brown with black spots all over, and it has the lovely habit of coming to the door of our house for a pat and a little snack. We admit that its snack is a little larger at times, especially after our hosts have served us meals. The women prepare all the meals, as Tongan men don't usually cook, and Malohi's wife, Emeni, seems to be the master cook in our family. While we appreciate her looking after us, and most meals are tasty, there are times when we can't bring ourselves to swallow what she cooks. So instead, we secretly feed it to Schweinchen. Returning food to our hosts would seriously offend them and counter our aim to be more accepted. We need to blame ourselves for being picky eaters, but an explanation of our daily cuisine is also required.

The earth oven is only used for cooking on Sundays. During the week, our hosts prepare the food in a basic fire pit outside the cooking house, surrounded by dirt, roaming pigs or dogs, and playing children. Thus, dirt and anything stuck to the animals' snouts is inadvertently added to the pot. Most meals are served in liquid coconut milk, and the coconut taste is so strong that it overpowers the taste of the meat cooked in it. We don't mind if this is beef or chicken but have yet to find a liking for dog or horse meat.

Preserved mutton flaps, locally called Sipi, are often on the menu. While we know many good things that originate from New Zealand, this is not one of them. It appears New Zealanders, after slaughtering their sheep, send to Tonga whatever cut-offs they don't find fit for consumption. Mutton flaps are the low-quality meat from the ends of a sheep's rib, containing about 40% fat. They are conserved in salt brine in large buckets and shipped off to the islands. The chunks of mutton are not only salty and fatty; they are also so tough that we would need an extra set of teeth for biting. In the absence of such luxury, Schweinchen enjoys those meals instead.

Occasionally, Malohi treats us to a different type of protein: octopus and turtle meat. One day, one of his sons goes spearfishing and catches a turtle. Malohi shows us its shell, and to us, the poor thing looks at least a few decades old. The patterns on the shell tell us that it is a Hawksbill Turtle, not a Green Sea Turtle, which also occurs here. These turtles are protected species, but here, they are food whenever someone can catch them in the sea nearby.

Fish is a rare visitor to our dinner plates as the rough sea is often not calm enough for spearfishing, and fishing with a line and hook from the shore is not a common pastime. At first, we are thrilled when Malohi's wife, Emeni, serves us fish one day, even though we could do without the coconut milk it swims in. But this thrill is dampened as soon as we taste the fish. For some unfathomable reason, she does not remove the gall bladder before cooking, which gives the dish such a disgusting bitter taste that we can only choke rather than swallow. Emeni would see any remark about her cooking as offensive and critical, so we instead have to make Schweinchen happy whenever fish is on the menu. Preparing the fish by ourselves is also not an option, as we have agreed to pay Malohi's family for food preparation, and it would hurt his pride if we did this ourselves instead.

Meat is always served with some kind of starchy side dish. We use the term "side dish" instead of "vegetable", as the main addition to most meals is breadfruit. Botanically speaking, this is a fruit, not a vegetable, though not of the sweet juicy kind. It contains lots of starch, like bread, hence the name. The 20-metre-or-so-high breadfruit trees don't need any care, and each tree produces about 200 fruit per season, making it a valuable food source for the locals. Here on this island, the rich volcanic soil provides all the nutrients for growth, and according to Malohi, the trees bear breadfruit all year round. The fruit looks like soccer balls with pimples and thick skin, and the abundance of the fruit makes shopping for dinner easy: Climb the tree, hurl down the fruit, throw the whole thing in the fire until the outer crust is completely burnt, then scoop out the soft flesh in the middle. For us, the only problem with this regular staple is that it has hardly any taste.

Before coming here, someone had told us that it tastes like potatoes or freshly baked bread, but maybe our sense of taste is too spoiled from German potato dishes and bread delicacies. For now, we have to accept that breadfruit will be our lunch and part of dinner for many months to come.

A change from breadfruit comes in the form of stumpy green bananas called hopas. These cooking bananas are relatively easy to grow and are harvested when still green. They are boiled in water and taste somewhat bland to us, except they contain some oxalic acid that scratches our throat like an abrasive scourer sponge. We would prefer them ripe and sweeter but have only received two ripe ones so far. The locals don't often let them ripen on the tree because they would be eaten by the introduced Indian Mynah birds instead. The recipe for hopas contains two options: cook in the earth oven or cook in a pot on the fire. We prefer the first, as it leaves the fruit relatively clean. On the contrary, when boiled in a large pot on the fire, the cooking water is inadvertently spiced with soil from the surrounding 'floor'.

While preparing for our trip, we read so much about the many different root vegetables that locals usually grow in the South Pacific. Accordingly, we had the wrong expectations that we would live off cassava (manioc), taro, sweet potato, and yams. Instead, breadfruit and cooking bananas are our staple diet. Occasionally we are served some cassava, as it is relatively easy to grow, but the other three types are only ever cooked on some weekends and feasts. The main reason seems to be that they require farming work and plantations that pigs do not destroy. Climbing a tree for breadfruit is much easier instead.

The only green vegetable that seems to exist on the island is called *Lu pulu* and is grown as hedges around the houses[1]. Emeni regularly adds these green leaves to our coconut meals. We know that greens are good for us, but this one contains so much oxalate (oxalic acid) that it stings our mouth, plus it is riddled with mucilage that leaves a very slimy feeling in our throat. Thus, despite the apparent health benefits of this super green, it too is mainly destined to end up in Schweinchen's belly.

For breakfast, we occasionally cook ourselves some carefully portioned oats and milk powder mixed with water on our little fuel stove. Our supplies are limited, and we also try to eat the breakfasts that Emeni cooks. Her speciality is *ceke*, which comes from the English name "cake". It is a name that does not quite live up to its promise, at least to us. Malohi has secured a big bucket of flour and an equally big bucket of beef tallow from the ship's supply. The flour is mixed with water and then deep-fried in tallow. No matter how hard we try, we feel very nauseous from the fat each time we eat this Tongan cake. It

---

1. Latin name most likely *Abelmoschus manihot*; in other parts of Polynesia this is called *Pele*.

is too valuable for Schweinchen, so we return it and make up a story that we prefer to eat oats in our culture.

We also naively expected to find much fruit in this tropical climate. This assumption is correct during September/October each year when the many mango trees bear fruit. They don't need watering or maintenance. Only a few people grow fruit that needs to be properly farmed, such as pineapple, or fruit growing on trees that require some care, such as pawpaw, custard apple, banana, or citrus fruit. During the first two weeks of our stay, the mangoes were still in season, and we undertook daily hikes to those trees to fill up on fruit. Now, we are forced to take vitamin pills, as our regular begging for fruit from the residents only yields intermittent success. The locals don't seem to eat much fruit either. They might even suffer from Vitamin C deficiency, as during a recent bout of bad weather, when the temperature dropped below 30 degrees Celsius, many of them started sneezing.

In the humid heat we live in, drinking is even more important than eating. The island's drinks menu contains two options: rainwater or coconut water from young coconuts. The latter is refreshing and often astonishingly cool, despite the oppressive heat outside. If only the coconuts were not separated from us by 10-metre or so tall trunks, and we didn't have to beg the local men to use their climbing skills and fetch them for us. Thus, water is our drink most of the time, and that too comes with some drawbacks. Springs or flowing creeks do not exist on the island, and the crater lake, far away from the village, only contains brackish water that is not suitable for drinking. So instead, the locals collect water for drinking or washing off the few tin roofs into concrete tanks. The nearest tank is next to a local church, a few houses down from us, so we carry bucket after bucket back to our hut for drinking and washing. Only once this week did Ivo make the mistake of drinking the water straight from the tank, which made him sick soon after. We now make sure to always prepare the water for drinking with our water disinfectant tablets and portable water filter apparatus.

After some weeks of drinking rainwater, we realise that we have not paid enough attention to one particular side effect of this drink: it does not contain many minerals. Drinking water only contains minerals if it has seeped through the soil, and rainwater hasn't had that chance. Our bodies need minerals, and their absence explains why we often feel so tired. Luckily we have brought mineral supplements, and now that we take these every day, we feel more energetic and can tolerate the constant high humidity of about 80%. On some days, in this sweltering misery, we give up on changing clothes repeatedly because they get drenched in sweat again anyway.

10

Head First Deep Down in a Burrow

During the following two weeks, we visit some of Malau's egg-laying grounds. We aim to carefully dig up some eggs, measure the depth, temperature, and soil humidity where we find them, and then return them to the burrow as we found them. We also add small pencil numbers to the shells so that when we later discover the shell fragments of hatched eggs, we can determine how long they have been incubated. Additionally, a simple candling device allows us to shine a light through the egg and determine how developed the embryo is.

We use a small shovel first to remove some of the soil. Then we need to use our hands to avoid damaging the eggs. It's hard and sweaty work, heads down in a burrow, and we have newfound admiration for Lakepi, who seems to do it with such ease. Taking turns helps, but the person on top also has to hold the digging person by the feet in case the burrow collapses and quick retrieval is necessary. Lakepi told us that one local man died when buried in a deep egg-laying burrow some twenty years ago.

While digging up other egg-laying burrows in the weeks to come, we ask ourselves why we would ever want to go to a sauna again, now that we have repeatedly stuck our heads into hot burrows like this. The temperature in the egg-laying burrows varies quite a lot. This variation is a good prerequisite for translocating the birds to a new island, as the new home may not have the same temperatures. We find eggs incubating anywhere between 29 and 35 degrees Celsius, and it is no surprise that we prefer to dig up those burrows within the 'cooler' range of these temperatures.

Digging up the eggs is also easier in those burrows where the eggs are not positioned quite as deep. These depths range anywhere from 20 to 130 cm, but eggs found in shallow depths may have been dug up by other Malau digging in the burrows. Many females use these sites communally, and there is competition for the best incubation spots. Those prime real estate burrows contain more eggs and soft soil, whereas some less favourable ones are filled with larger pebbles and roots, making it hard for the females or chicks to dig. Unfortunately, those inferior burrows are where we occasionally find rotten eggs that force us to leave the area in no time. The putrid smell of rotten eggs combined with the heat and humidity is a bit much to bear, even for the most enthusiastic of field biologists.

While our expeditions aim to find the Malau, we also try to take note of all the other species of animals and plants we find. Many plants inhabit this island with its fertile volcanic soil, but no Westerner has yet identified which ones occur here. So far, all our guides—Laione, Kailao, and Lakepi—have impressed us with their knowledge of local vegetation. They know the Tongan names of many species, and if there is one they don't know, we take it home and usually rely on Malohi to identify it. Luckily, we have a dictionary of Tongan and English plant names that a botanist created years ago, enabling us to compile a list of plants encountered.

Identifying animals, at least the vertebrates, is much easier, as there aren't many. Like so many islands isolated in the Pacific, Niuafo'ou is not inhabited by many vertebrates. They simply didn't manage to get here unless they could fly well, were blown over in a storm, or could hang onto some driftwood or a boat. We find only three species of mammals: two bats and the small Polynesian rat. There are a few more reptiles. I am fascinated that somehow eight species of skinks and geckos made it to this remote island by hanging onto driftwood or boats[1]. Birds are more numerous. So far, we have discovered 14 breeding species but are still in the process of finding more. We are most pleased not to encounter two species of larger rats that have caused havoc when introduced to other islands worldwide: Black and Brown rats (*Rattus norvegicus* and *Rattus rattus*). These two rats threaten local reptiles and birds wherever they appear, as they eat them or their eggs and breed prolifically. Niuafo'ou might have been spared from their invasion because it does not have a harbour, meaning big ships, which often carry these rats, can't land on the island, and the pests don't have a chance to hop ashore. For the Malau, their introduction

---

1. Gill, B.J. and Rinke, D.R. (1990). Records of Reptiles from Tonga. *Records of the Auckland Institute and Museum*, 27: 175-180.

would be detrimental, and we keep a note to include that in our conservation plan for this species.

A chance arises to talk to the kids at the local high school, offered by the Tongan teacher who is from outside Niuafo'ou and quite interested in our work. We pitch our message about conserving the Malau for future generations at their level of understanding, which triggers exciting discussions among themselves in the Tongan language. We can only guess what they say, as the students mostly understand our English but are not willing to reply in this language. One or two, though, ask a question that seems to reflect what many of them think. Why on Earth would we want to come from the other side of the world to study a bird? Why leave a world where you can have corned beef every day to live on this breadfruit-dominated island? We try our best to justify this decision but are unsure how successful we are. Our explanation centres around conserving an endangered species, but we can see from their blank looks that our reasoning does not convince our audience.

11

Ofato Grubs and Kava

On Sunday, the kids offer us a local delicacy. While the youngsters approach, their hands outstretched, several adults watch us from afar with giggling smiles. The offered treat is a bunch of *Ofato*, large wriggling larvae of a longhorn beetle that the kids have collected from inside dead trees, where the beetle larvae feed on rotten wood. Like the Aboriginals in Australia who eat similar Witchetty Grubs, Tongans also devour these white larvae full of protein. The kids demonstrate how to eat them alive: stick the rear end in your mouth and start biting it off while the head, including the mandible mouthparts, still wriggles outside your lips. Occasionally, the grubs might also bite your tongue or excrete tiny pellets of digested wood pulp. We know that locals would accept us more if we ate these, but the snack is just a bit too gross. If we ate these, we might as well slurp on slimy worms, so we decline with a smile, accompanied by the laughter of the adults nearby. A bit later, some young men come over to talk to Ivo about the *Ofato* casually. It becomes evident that these finger-thick larvae are both a local delicacy and a symbol for the penis. Joking about it seems to be some male bonding ritual, and after the men have left, full of laughter, we are not sure whether Ivo has fooled around with them enough and passed the bonding test.

The men also ask Ivo to join activities that I, as a woman, am not allowed to participate in. The first is an evening Kava ceremony. These occur almost every night and function as a social lubricant for men. Only one woman who serves the Kava drink is allowed in this ceremony. She has to be unmarried and not related to any of the men participating, as this would make it impossible to talk openly, especially about politics and courtship. Talking becomes easier once the Kava drink loosens the tongue. Kava is produced from the crushed, chewed (yes, chewed!) and ground root and stump of a local shrub from the pepper family of plants, mixed with water. The men drink it from coconut cups passed from hand to hand while talking and singing for hours. At first, this drug makes them feel happier, relaxed, and sleepy, and as consumption increases, it can cause drowsiness. Ivo later reports that some of the men in his group seemed to be asleep for a large part of the evening. He mainly experienced a numb mouth and throat, a common side effect, and he found the drink rather unpleasant. He sat cross-legged through the night, talking and joking as much as he could, hoping that his participation would help him become more accepted by the local men.

The men also enjoy teasing Ivo about his inability to climb coconut palms. We admire them when they almost fly up those tall vertical stems of coconut palms, ten or more metres high. Their only aid is a machete which they use to hack steps into the stem and cut off the coconuts from their tree. The nuts hit the ground with a loud 'plonk' before people use them as essential food for themselves, their pigs, horses, and dogs. They cook most meals in milk made by squeezing the flesh of ripe coconuts, and they regularly drink the water from inside the young ones. While climbing the trees is not within our ability, we have at least learned how to open the young coconuts like the locals do, with three machete hits. It took a lot of practice, but we now manage to create a nice round hole in the shell, just the right size to drink from. Maybe this skill will help us be more accepted by the locals.

Sitting cross-legged is a skill we should have practised more at home. It is the key to participating in Kava ceremonies and many other social gatherings. Unfortunately, elevated seating opportunities only exist at church; otherwise, people sit on the floor, cross-legged, often on woven pandanus mats. One day, we are invited to a feast in a neighbouring village. Several beautifully woven mats create a rectangle on the floor. Food such as chunks of meat, root vegetables, and watermelon is laid out on banana leaves in the middle of the mats, covered with a fly net and nicely decorated with hibiscus flowers. People of higher social position and age sit closest to the food while those of lower social rank take their places on the perimeter. A lady in a colourful dress asks us to sit down somewhere in between, and we feel privileged to join such a traditional feast, exchanging smiles and basic phrases with the locals. I am glad to have worn a dress as all the ladies do, even though I am not wearing a traditional *ta'ovala*, a woven skirt, around my waist. The ladies' *ta'ovalas* are a work of art, beautifully woven and embellished. One of them tells me it is made of the inner bark of the Fanakio tree (*Sterculia fanahio*), which is better for creating fine mats than the leaves of the pandanus tree. In Tonga, it can only be found on this island.

One of the ladies passes me a hibiscus flower to wear over my ear, and I follow this tradition like all the women around me do. They always place hibiscus or frangipani flowers over one ear on festive occasions, but it is crucial to know the secret code. A flower behind your left ear means you are either married, taken, or have a special someone in your life. Right-eared flowers signal that you are still free, so women need to carefully consider whether they want to send this message to the men nearby. Unless they are ready to mingle, they usually prefer to leave it on the left side and maybe quickly switch it over should the right contestant be nearby.

We enjoy the feeling of being accepted and the food, eaten with bare hands as Tongans usually do. When invited to help ourselves from the banana leaves, we grab some of the juicy chunks of pork and root vegetables, including the valued yams. The watermelon, in particular, is a welcome refreshing treat, the first time we have encountered one on this island. In our communication with the locals, I also notice that I have become more fluent in the non-verbal signals that the Tongans use so frequently. Smiles are part of this, but even more important is the quick but emphatic raising of eyebrows that I now automatically employ when signalling a yes or approval of what another person says. My only problem today is that I can't sit cross-legged for the whole two hours of the feast. After an hour or so, I try to move my numb legs to the side secretly, but this does not go unnoticed. Immediately, one of the older women reprimands me sternly: "Ana, sit right." Oh dear, now I feel less accepted by the local women again.

12

A Phone Expedition

We need to get in touch with Mr Hopps, hoping he will send us some more supplies with the next ship and discuss some details of our research permit and work. The only way to do so is to make a phone call from the one phone booth on the island. As it turns out, this is a sort of social entertainment hub where many people venture just to find out what's going on. The process of making a phone call requires some getting used to. First, one has to walk there at 7 am to register a phone call, then return late morning to make the actual call. I plan to walk the 10 minutes to the booth by myself, but Laveni, Malohi's daughter, quickly points out that this is against Tongan etiquette. Women don't walk around in public alone and must always accompanied by another woman, partner, or a male relative.

Laveni readily volunteers to come along as this gives her potential story material for later on. Meanwhile, I ponder what I have learnt about the role of women in Tongan society. Yes, they are highly respected and have a lot to say, but at the same time, they are not allowed to walk anywhere by themselves and are expected to do all the cooking, household chores, and tending to the children. This gender role is not quite the emancipated idea I had in mind when Susan in Nuku'alofa described Tongan society as a matriarchal society to me. Obviously, my associations were not correct.

My estimate of a 10-minute walking time to the phone booth does not allow for the time-consuming conversations that one needs to have on the way. Each time we meet another person, we exchange smiles, and then the encountered person asks, "*Ko ho'o 'alú ki fē?*"—Where do you go? You then utter the name of a village down the road, upon which you hear back, "*Ana 'alu ai*"—Ana you go there. The final bit of the conversation consists of me saying a long-drawn "*Iooooo*"—yes. We meet many people and exchange this conversation each time. Quite a few of them are initially heading in the opposite direction but then turn around and follow us upon hearing that we are venturing to the social hub. A pālangi is talking—that might be worthwhile listening to!

The person who talks on the phone creates story material for the others by talking so loudly that everyone nearby can hear what they say. Loud talking is necessary because the connection through the two-way radio is so bad that only yelling into the receiver results in some kind of communication. Much to the amusement of the onlookers, I first don't realise that I have to press a button on the side of the receiver to talk and then release it at the right time to listen to the other person. There are some dusty headphones available, but nobody seems to put them on anyway. Using them would mean that you have something to hide and would fuel the village gossip even more. Also, you would take away the entertainment for the onlookers, who nod when they agree with what they hear, laugh when the phone user laughs, and repeatedly add their comments to what is being said.

My audience must be disappointed when I take away their story material by talking to Mr Hopps in German, whereas I am more than disappointed by what I hear from Mr Hopps. It appears that he and the Professor have now disagreed about the details of the project, and he wants us to return to the main island to finish the application for our research visas ourselves. Mr Hopps doesn't care that we are 600 km away, on an island with unpredictable flight connections, and these tickets would eat up a large chunk of our funds. Moreover, our tourist visas will expire soon, and this situation thus leaves us in the lurch. When I ask him to please send some essential supplies on the next ship, Mr Hopps asks why we need flour and crackers if we can find so many coconuts to eat. This remark doesn't amuse me, given our limited food choices on this island.

The most disappointing news is that Mr Hopps now also wants us to catch some birds for his zoo, a job that he has never mentioned to us before. One of these birds is a beautiful small parrot, the Blue-crowned lory. Not only do we disagree with catching birds for captivity, but these colourful beauties also live high up in the coconut palms. Catching them would require difficult climbing and installing nets high up, which would take up most of our time. We are seething with anger, and it looks like we have no choice but to return to the main island in a month, solve our visa issues, and get some essential supplies. At least we can add some chocolate then because poor Ivo is starting to dream of such delicacies. In tiny letters, much smaller than the other writing, he has added the word 'chocolate' to our shopping list.

13

Big Fat or Small Fat?

Most villagers go to church two or three times each Sunday, constantly going back and forth between church, meals, and sleep all day. We attend once, and one Sunday, Kailao asks us to join him in his Wesleyan church. The preacher reads the Bible passages with zeal and works himself into such an excited state that he starts to cry. Tears in public are nothing special in Tonga. We remember that when the Moana left Nuku'alofa on the mainland, the harbour was full of people who waved goodbye and cried loudly, and the people travelling with us shed a lot of tears as well. For today's sermon, Kailao has kindly marked the correct passages in the Bible for us. It is a nice gesture, but it is all in Tongan and somewhat hard to follow. So instead, we secretly glance around to take in the atmosphere.

My attention is drawn to the many children who have to come along to the church. Some little ones are asleep on the benches, and others muck around on the floor. If one gets too loud, an adult pulls them outside and hands out some slaps to teach them the seriousness of church. Sleeping babies are passed from one person to another, and I can't understand how they keep sleeping in all that noise, especially when the resonating singing of the women starts.

After the sermon, a young woman dances the traditional dance in front of the church community. It is not the Hula belly dance many people associate with the South Sea but a dignified and graceful combination of slow arm movements, elegant head tilting, and occasional foot-stomping. To us, it seems to echo ancient times. Part of the dance custom is the acknowledgement by onlookers, who traditionally presented the dancer with mats and tapa fabric. Today, the church uses this dance for collecting money. The dancer has rubbed coconut oil all over her bare arms, and each church community member has to come forward and stick some money in notes to the skin. Peer pressure causes people to give as much as they can, as everyone is watching, and they don't want to appear stingy, even if they have little to offer.

Kailao has already told us how much money he pays to the church. About 250 Pa'anga dollars per year, which is almost one month's worth of salary for him. As a policeman, he earns 280 Pa'anga a month, of which he pays 130 to pay off his house, another large amount as a school fee for his four kids, and taxes also need to be paid, even on Niuafo'ou. Apart from the monthly church fee, additional money donations are expected during every Sunday service, and as we experience, everyone checks that others contribute correctly. No wonder people here never have any money.

Not many here have a proper waged job like Kailao unless they are one of the few other government representatives or manage to sell a bit of copra or vanilla to the mainland now and then. Most people live off the land—coconuts are their lifeline as they provide food for themselves and their pigs, dogs and horses. Breadfruit is the other life support, supplemented by a few farmed crops and fishing. The bit of cash they have and the nice clothes they own mainly come from members of their family living in other parts of Tonga or overseas. With so many children born, most families have one relative either in more affluent parts of Tonga or, if they are lucky, in New Zealand, Australia, or the US. For a young woman here, marrying someone from those countries is the most cherished dream, and Laveni has already asked us whether we know someone in Germany who may want to marry her. She may have been joking, but maybe not; we aren't sure but will not act as a dating agency, that's for sure. Those who manage to emigrate then send home whatever money they can spare, as sharing is a big part of Tongan culture. As a result, many families rely heavily on the remittance sent by their relatives overseas.

After church, we meet many locals while people stand around and chat for long periods—the church is clearly the social hub of the village. Back at the hut, Kailao and Malohi regularly pass by to talk. Malohi seems to warm up to us. The reserved facial expressions we first saw in this proud elder are now more often replaced by a genuine and friendly smile. He takes pride in teaching us his language and seeing our praise for the food he serves. In Tongan, he has recently started talking to us about his *hokohoko*, his ancestors, and how proud he is that they too had the status of local chiefs. Genealogy seems extremely important to many Tongans, and Kailao has also mentioned to us that one of his ancestors was a famous politician in Tonga. Whenever we run out of topics to talk about, there is always the wriggly Ofato caterpillar to help raise some laughter. "This island is famous for Ofato," Kailao proudly tells us, followed by, "The king eats a whole plate of Ofato when he visits every year or two."

Another common topic for our joint jokes is that we are both not big enough, and we need to get away from our small status. If only we had the odd bar of chocolate to help us in this endeavour! Tongans' ideal body image is shifted towards larger bodies, which might have a long history. We read that in pre-Christian times, people performed a puberty ritual called 'fattening' in some Polynesian societies. They secluded male and female youths for some time, kept them out of direct sunlight and inactive, and fed them large amounts of food to make them more sexually desirable.

Both Kailao and Malohi seem happy that we are interested in *Anga Faka-Tongá*, the Tongan way of life. They enjoy explaining various parts of their customs and traditions to us, especially Kailao, who speaks good English. He is also very interested in our culture and asks lots of questions. "Why in your land do some people own more than others?" he asks. "Here we all share with the big family, all we have. Give help and then get help back when we need it," he adds. Unfortunately, we don't have a satisfying simple explanation to offer for our society's individualistic and less group-oriented approach to wealth. Later, when by ourselves, we discuss how different our society would look if we too detested those who do not share or prioritise their personal interests over that of the group.

Malohi's daughter Laveni now visits more often too, and quite frequently, she silently sits on our doorstep for a long time. Her name, by the way, comes from the English word Lavender. We are unsure what to do with her, as she either does not speak much English or does not want to converse. It appears to us that she is not here to see us but rather to be a bit closer to the lava stone house next door. The bachelors in that house also spend considerable time outside their entry door. Both they and Laveni send frequent glances and smiles to each other. In Tongan society, the elders strictly separate young men and women, and it seems Laveni, aged 18, has found a way to bypass that control from above.

I manage to get some information out of Laveni while she sits there. It has intrigued us to find out who is who in Falaki's large family, as our confusion increased when Laveni sometimes talked about Emeni as her mother but later named a different woman as her mum. "All my family," Laveni says when I point to all the houses nearby. Family and kinship ties are so important in Tongan culture. It appears that this is Malohi's extended family, and Laveni refers to all her maternal aunts as 'mother' and all paternal uncles as 'father'. She also seems to think of her cousins as her brothers and sisters. The young children, who are no longer afraid of us, are raised by extended family members, and we are not even sure who their actual parents are. Laveni told me that the mother of at least one of the little girls lives in the US and sends home money to sustain the family.

Once Laveni leaves, we have some young men as visitors. They hum and haw for a while before asking us for cigarette paper, offering to pay later. Unfortunately, soon after the ship's arrival, many of them have run out of tobacco and cigarette paper again, and they have to revert to smoking the crunched leaves of a local tree rolled up in cigarette paper. We hand out a few sheets of paper each time, knowing that they will never be able to pay us anyway, but we can't be too generous as this would soon lead to an influx of such visitors. Luckily, the overall number of people asking for our goods is limited as we stand under the protection of Malohi and Kailao, both highly regarded men.

The bachelors in the house next door still have enough batteries to operate a tape recorder, from which they play the one cassette tape they own—again and again. It contains a version of 'Jingle Bells' sung in Tongan. Initially grateful for this cultural delight, we soon start to hope the batteries would run out. With our ears threatening to split, we eventually lend them the two cassette tapes we brought along. A compilation containing songs by Pink Floyd and others is not such a hit with them, but they love a whole tape with songs by the Argentine singer Mercedes Sosa with her deep penetrating voice. The children come over and dance along, and we all enjoy the happy atmosphere. Obviously, Mercedes sounds similar to the local women when they sing their a cappella songs with such fervour, especially in church.

14

Volcanic Powers

We have spent a lot of time in the dense and humid jungle and now fancy a change of scenery. Our destination is the lava fields that cover much of the southwestern part of the island, near the shore. Walking here feels almost surreal, so far removed from the rest of the world. We admire the beautiful colour contrast of the black lava against the lush green vegetation and the bright blue sea.

We venture deeper into one of the black lava fields and feel as if we are either in a *Back to the Future* movie or a documentary on the immense potency of Mother Earth. The lava that erupted in 1946 had slowly flowed from the caldera to the sea, often cooling down before it reached the water. The patterns we now see in the solid lava show us the direction in which the lava had travelled and where it had stopped. The colours indicate the size of those lava streams; in the thicker streams, the outermost dark black is in stark contrast to the reddish-brown of the interior. Except for the odd fern, no plants have managed to take hold in this barren area. In this grim, lifeless field of desolation, we have to choose our steps carefully, as in some areas, the lava is so thin that we could easily break in and cut our legs on the rugged edge.

Our path crosses the former village of Angaha, largely destroyed during the last volcanic eruption in 1946. All we can find now are some stone steps that lead to nowhere, obviously the former entrance of a house. Among all the lava rubble, we detect an old rusty benchtop clock that has stopped at 8:30 am. It might have been owned by a missionary, as Tongans here don't use many watches or clocks. We pull a book out of our backpack that we bought on the main island. It is entitled *The Fire has Jumped*[1], and today, we want to read the story it contains at the place where it originated. The story describes the last volcanic eruption and was written by Sister Mary Julia of the Catholic Mission shortly after the event. Ivo sits down on some lava rocks and, with a dramatic tone, reads the story aloud to me: "*The tragic event occurred on Monday, September 9th at 7:30 pm after an hour of earth tremors and quakes and shakes. We had counted 27 really good ones. Father was making kava on his veranda with a few natives who, looking towards Piu and 'Ahau where the 1943 eruption had occurred, unanimously declared that there was no danger. Had they glanced northward and noticed how the sky looked over the rocky coast, they would have let the kava bowl drop down at once. A crash and a boom-boom were heard behind the house towards the sea. All the while the 'atomic bombs' were popping out at a distance. The noise of the sea, the detonations from the rocky coast, all were deafening. We went to our rooms and got busy pulling a mat from the bed. A blanket and all was tumbling down in the rush. While we were packing, the heat was getting to be unbearable. The fire had jumped and was running our way. There was no time to lose or we would be buried alive. When we passed the corner of the church, I happened to turn my head towards the landing. What I saw was enough to turn anyone into an icy ball. A pillar of fire and clouds of smoke with pieces of fire bouncing up and falling on every side. All seemed to be running full speed towards us. Lightning flashed and muttering thunder sounded through the air and continually grew louder. The atmosphere was heavy with the odour of sulphur—a mouthful swallowed while jumping over the fence was choking me. We followed Taipaleti up and up the steep, sheer perpendicular slope, as difficult to climb as a coconut tree. The next morning from Piu Heights we had a view of the village of Angaha. Horrible to see, the town had turned into a lava field. The radio station, no trace of it! The post office was a belching crater; the postmaster's house a piece of molten lava. Copra sheds were burning slowly. Where was the Government school? Gone too under the piled-up lava. Scattered along the coast from Pulei to Kekei were craters shaped like Christmas puddings, fire and steam still puffing out of them. But miracle of miracle, the Catholic Church was still standing untouched, surrounded by craters and smoking lava fields. We ventured into the town to try to rescue our belongings, walking stealthily and in great trepidation, fearing at every step to disappear into one of those wide-open fiery mouths belching on every side. At every detonation, the earth opened*

---

1. Garth, R. (Ed.). (1986). *The Fire has Jumped—Eye-witness accounts of the eruption and evacuation of Niuafo'ou, Tonga.* Suva, Fiji: University of the South Pacific, Institute of Pacific Studies.

somewhere. I paused in front of the church. Suddenly, deafening noise and a stream of red, overwhelming fumes spewed in the air. Behind the church another crash was heard, and the ground opened at my feet. We were in real danger. That memorable night of the 10th of September was to be still worse than the night before. Up on the heights of Piu we all slept on mats on the ground. All of a sudden there was a noise like half a dozen cannons roaring at the same time and then monster volcanoes buried under the sea began to pour out tons and tons of red-hot stones, sulphur, and lava. What a sight it was to see fire coming out of the water! A dozen big mouths spitting out fire from midnight until 7 am Wednesday morning."

The story leaves a deep impression on us, and we sit in silence after re-reading these lines at the actual scene of the events. Poor people who have lived through this horrific experience! Sister Mary's account also tells us that the Catholic church may still be standing. "Let's go search for it," my adventure-loving boyfriend exclaims. We systematically comb the vegetation next to the lava field as if we are looking for some lost valuables. Finally, there it is: a ruin of stone walls with some window openings and the church tower still recognisable, though without a roof and almost completely overgrown by vines. This scene would make a good backdrop for a horror film or something similarly eerie.

After this last eruption, the Tongan government decided it was too dangerous to live on Niuafo'ou. By December 1946, it had forcefully evacuated all 1,300 inhabitants and resettled them on the Tongan island of 'Eua, far to the south. The locals were rounded up and forced to board the ships in a military-style operation. However, some resourceful islanders managed to hide when the evacuation crew arrived, and they remained for the next 12 years without the authorities' knowledge. They were only joined by more people in 1958 when the first 200 original inhabitants were officially allowed to return from 'Eua to their home island.

For now, all we can hope is that the volcano beneath us will not have another of its explosive outbursts. We find some distraction from such sombre thoughts at one of the patches that contain coconuts: 'Tongan Ice Cream'. Kailao recently showed us how to find this culinary delight in coconuts that have to be at exactly the right stage of development. When ripe, these nuts have fallen off the tree and have started sending out a shoot that would later become a tree. At this stage of development, the coconut water has transformed into a spongy white substance that is quite sweet and can be revealed with a hit of the machete. With a bit of imagination, we can compare it to ice cream or candy floss.

Lured by the prospect of more Tongan ice cream, we swing our machete to clear our way through some more shrubs. Unfortunately, this proves to be a mistake, as we disturb a nest of giant hornets that immediately attack us in large numbers. They come from all sides and manage to sting us several times before we have run far enough to evade them. Ouch, the stings hurt, and all we can do is apply ointment from our first aid kit and wait for the pain to subside. The joy of ice cream is gone. Later that day, we learn from Kailao that these hornets only appeared on the island a few years ago. They must have flown in during a storm from nearby Samoa, where they are common and have been introduced to combat the flies. Their nest looks like a small umbrella hanging on a string and is hidden within some low shrubs. This makes it hard to find the nest, and it is easy to get stung when you try to venture through shrubby areas. I am now slightly less fascinated by the topic of chance on islands—specifically, which animals accidentally manage to arrive here. These critters don't deserve that chance!

15

Lake on the Islet in the Lake on the Island in the Sea

It is mid-October 1991, and after six weeks of staying in the village, we realise that we need to live closer to the birds to solve more Malau puzzles. We have yet to set eyes on the adult birds for long enough to observe them properly. Motu Molemole, one of the islands in the crater lake, is an ideal place for such an undertaking as it contains a good-sized population of Malau, and locals don't visit it often. It takes some patience to convince Malohi and Kailao that we will be safe and that the *tevolo*—devil—that many locals fear at night won't be out there to get us. Their fear of the devil is not superficial; it seems to sit deep within them and may have either been instilled by the missionaries or is a relic of a more ancient belief system from the times before missionaries arrived. During those old times, Tongans believed in a sky god and a god of the underworld, and maybe the *tevolo* represents the latter. Also, according to our guidebook, many Tongans still believe in the taboos, spirits, and superstitions of pre-Christian Polynesia. The *tevolo* might be one of those spirits for them.

After much discussion with our host, he finally agrees that we can leave during the week, as long as we return to Esia every Sunday. We are relieved to have obtained his official permission. In Tongan society, people of lower social rank, even pālangi, are expected to demonstrate respect and obedience to those of higher status. It would not look good in this status-conscious society if we left the village every week against the will of the chief and the policeman.

By now, sleeping in a tent on Motu Molemole is a more appealing option than our palm-frond hut in the village, which isn't such a romantic place to live after all. Mosquitos love to hide in it, and we are still surprised when they pester us with such shocking rapacity. They find swimming pools for their larvae in the many empty coconut shells that lie around everywhere. Apart from the one centipede, we have luckily encountered no more of them, but there are plenty of Polynesian rats, cockroaches, and wood borers to occupy us instead. The latter work their way through the poles that hold up our roof, and we can hear their gnawing noise at night. A spider, the size of our hand, sits on our ceiling, and after some discussion about whether she might be a friend or poisonous foe, we have decided to leave her alone as she may catch some of the mosquitos, flies, and cockroaches for us.

We start our trip to Motu Molemole with renewed vigour, lots of equipment, our last few dry Pacific cracker biscuits, and corned beef stored in our backpack barrels. In one hand, we both carry a basket full of breadfruit and cooking bananas, in the other, a canister of drinking water. Our path first takes us up to the crater rim, then down the steep path through the dense jungle to the lake, from where we swim across to our new weekday home. Establishing camp near the crater lake doesn't take long, as all we have is our tent, three solar panels, two barrels to sit on, and a tarp to collect drinking water when it rains. Some lava stones serve as a border for cooking our first meal on a fire pit. If only the damp firewood didn't make it so hard to start the fire. We clearly need to collect and dry some wood under our tarp.

In the evening, just before dark, the sounds from the forest surprise us. A chorus of unknown birds, which we have never heard before, sings beautifully from the trees, responding to each other. We are even more astounded when using our binoculars to identify the singers. They are not songbirds, but Malau! Nobody knew that these chicken-like birds have such delightful calls and respond in this way to each other. With our microphone and Walkman in hand, we record what we hear. This becomes the first of many recordings, and Ivo decides there and then that it would be the foundation for his Master's thesis in years to come.

While we have now seen Malau in trees, we have yet to encounter one in the forest during the day. These birds look like brown and grey chickens with short tails, and they are timid and elusive. We are thrilled when we finally manage to slowly sneak up on a pair foraging on the forest floor. The two seem male and female, but we can't tell for sure as both sexes look alike. The only indication is the gentleman-like behaviour of one, presumably the male. He scratches around until he finds a grub, then steps aside to let the female pick it up.

We dedicate our first days on Motu Molemole to two crucial tasks: creating paths and a hide. The understorey is thick, and so far, our walking is often replaced by swinging our way from branch to branch like monkeys, crawling through fallen trees on our knees, and sliding down from the small crater rim on our bottom. After three days, our pants are already starting to wear out, making path creation an even more urgent task. While we diligently cut paths that serve the observation of the Malau, we make one that is mainly for recreation. It leads to the small crater lake on our islet, which shimmers in turquoise colours and invites us to swim.

"Yeah," Ivo calls out with delight as he plunges into the lake, "the lake on the islet on the lake on the island in the sea!" We have finally reached this fascinating landscape feature shaped by several volcanic eruptions. The first eruption created Niuafo'ou. Many years later, the volcanic cone collapsed in on itself, and rainwater filled the centre to form the large crater lake. Many more years later still, subsequent smaller volcanic eruptions started underneath this central crater lake. The resulting volcanic cones formed two smaller islets within the large lake, one with its miniature crater lake. This waterhole is where we are swimming now, and the experience is so unique that it justifies opening up our only bottle of wine. We sip it while immersed in the refreshing wet, feeling more removed from the rest of the world than we have ever felt before.

One of our sweaty tasks is to erect a hide near one of the more extensive egg-laying grounds of the Malau. My attempt at weaving coconut mats lags far behind what the local ladies can create but is good enough to make mats that we can use as walls for our hide. Ivo erects four corner posts, and we tie the mats to these with some string that we have made out of the bark of the hibiscus tree—a skill that Lakepi has taught us. From this hide, we will be able to watch the behaviour of the birds when they come to lay their one egg and, most importantly, establish how often individual females lay. These observations will be vital for assessing their ability to reproduce and maintain the population.

For the latter task, though, we need to identify individual females, and as they all look alike, we need to attach leg bands to them. This banding requires catching the birds, which leads to our next big task: building traps. Lakepi has shown us how the locals catch the birds with a noose made of bark that is turned into a string and then intricately attached to some sticks. The unfortunate Malau that steps onto these sticks soon has a noose tightened around its leg. The tension released in another thin stick pulls it up into the air, where the bird hangs upside down until collected. Of course, this is not what we want to achieve, but we adapt the trigger mechanism used by the locals so that the string instead closes a door of a two-metre-wide dome-like netted tent after the birds have entered. They can continue to scratch for food in this tent until our regular checks of the traps, and we can release them happy and healthy as soon as we have measured and banded them. Each bird receives some coloured leg bands of a unique colour combination and a wing tag with a letter and number combination. The design of our trap sounds like a good plan, but it takes two weeks and several alterations to our design before we can catch our first Malau.

We dutifully return to Esia on Saturdays for Sunday church, re-bonding with the locals and restocking our supplies. Usually, we walk, but on one particular Saturday, we arrange with Malohi to pick us up with his tractor near the crater rim. We arrive there a bit late, flustered from climbing up the steep path with our barrels on our backs. Being late in Tonga is not an issue, as everything runs on relaxed Tongan Time. Malohi and a few youngsters await us with a refreshing coconut in hand, and we can tell from his facial expressions that he is proud of us. At the same time, he grabs my arm muscles, squeezes them, and shakes his head. His gesture conveys that I don't fit the typical idea of a Tongan woman, as they are not supposed to carry heavy loads and bash through the bush as we do.

While sitting on the trailer, on our way to Esia, we think that we can hear a plane circling over the island. Perhaps our ears are playing tricks on us, and we are starting to imagine things in this quiet place, where nature sounds are our only entertainment. However, in Esia, we find we can trust our ears. A bundle of letters delivered by the plane awaits us, together with a bucket of Tongan water crackers that Mr Hopps's wife Susan has kindly sent. What a treat the dry crackers are, and how good it is to receive news from home!

Coming back to the village is a stern reminder of how desperate the people are for certain goods and how difficult it is to have some of those things while they don't. Laveni comes over and asks us in her broken English: "Ana, she gives for the salt?" After some prodding, we find out that one of their pigs has died, and they don't have any salt to preserve the meat. I hand over a large portion of our salt, hoping that we will be able to restock the supplies in the not-too-distant future. Soon after, Malohi tells us that they need some sugar, and after some hesitation, he swallows his pride and asks for tobacco for a cigarette, as he has run out. We would love to give him more than the bit he asks for to avoid this awkward situation in the future, but we need tobacco to trade for food, as money is currently of little use when there is nothing to buy on the island.

Back on Motu Molemole, we are proud that we have now somehow mastered two survival skills on this islet: fetching coconuts and avoiding hornet bites. Ivo can't believe his luck when he finds two coconut palms that have somehow grown nuts before shooting up. Without having to climb the tree, we can twist these welcome drink supplies off their stems with the aid of a long-forked stick. Also, we no longer instinctively run away during hornet encounters but rather stay completely still, in whatever position we were when we first heard the alarming buzz. This position may be standing on one leg or halfway through a stride. As uncomfortable as it sounds, it stops the insects from seeing and stinging us. We remember from our lectures in zoology that hornets and bees have compound eyes that can only detect motion. And indeed, when we freeze like a statue, they buzz around us but hardly ever sting. It may take ten frustrating minutes before they retreat, but it is worth the gymnastic exercise to avoid the bites.

We need to catch and mark more Malau on Motu Molemole during the next few weeks to understand their behaviour better. Hence, we require additional help with building our laborious tent traps. We couldn't hire anybody in Malohi's family as they are unlikely to resist the temptation of digging up the Malau eggs in their spare time. After listening to our concerns, Kailao recommends one young man as trustworthy, and we employ him after agreeing on a salary that includes money and tobacco. This recommendation gets us in big trouble with Malohi, as it hurts his pride and social status that we don't engage someone from his clan. In the village, Malohi provides us with the best food he can still afford, but it is clear that he does not want us to go into the field with this new assistant. First, our host refuses to give us our weekly allowance of starchy vegetables and young coconuts for the field altogether. The following week, he provides a small amount in a small basket that seems to have been woven especially small for this educational purpose.

Our new assistant carries the appropriate name Tokoni, which translates into 'a helper'. He seems to work to a schedule only known to himself, i.e., in Tongan Time—he arrives late, sits around for a while before commencing work and has long breaks. The traps he builds are useless for us as they contain too many holes and could harm the Malau. Moreover, he does sneak off once to dig up a Malau egg. We have to be careful not to reprimand him too much as we can't afford to make enemies among the young people. So far, we are under the protection of Malohi and Kailao, but if we make enemies, these youngsters could quickly decide to visit and bother us more often. After two weeks of difficulties with Malohi and Tokoni, we have had enough. It is time to put our foot down. We offer Kailao to pay him for root vegetables instead of our host, and this quickly reigns in Malohi. He changes his attitude and behaves as if nothing ever happened. Finally, we release Tokoni from his duties with the excuse that he has helped us so much and that we can now manage the work independently.

We also study the Malau chicks during our weeks on Motu Molemole, especially whether they can find all their food independently without watching other Malau. We have brought a small portable incubator which we power with batteries charged through our solar panels. Our candling technique, which involves shining a light through the egg, helps us identify an egg close to hatching, and we place the egg in the soil inside the incubator. What a joy to watch the first chick hatch! It doesn't hatch with its beak first, as all other birds do, but with its legs. That makes perfect sense when you hatch in the soil and have to kick free a tiny cavity to breathe in. Hatching legs first is not the only adaptation to underground hatching. We also find that the little creature has small jelly-like caps around his claws, which later fall off. This addition makes sense as it stops him from hurting himself with his sharp claws while kicking so furiously in the soil. His feathers are all completely enclosed in a coating made of keratin, also called a feather sheath, and as the chick is still very wet from all the fluids in the egg, the sheath prevents the feathers from becoming a muddy mess when underground.

It takes the chick about three hours to free itself from the eggshell in the soil, and a lot of heavy breathing and kicking are involved. It then takes another five hours for the soaking wet chick to dry and for its feathers to emerge from their coating. All of this would usually take place buried in the soil, and I would love to find out how they manage down there and how long it takes them to emerge from their underground nest. We have found a few chicks in burrows close to their eggshell, already completely dry and with their feathers emerged. This condition indicates that they rest for quite a while after hatching before they dig themselves out.

Once dry, we place the chick in a small aviary built from netting and wire, on the forest floor where it would usually live. And indeed, as soon as it has dried and rested after hatching, it starts scratching for food. We keep it for three more weeks before releasing it back into the forest, feeding it daily with termites, other grubs, and forest fruit. This period provides me with fascinating insights into the chicks' behaviour and growth. For example, during the first three days of keeping the fluffball, I am concerned because it becomes lighter instead of putting on weight, despite eating a lot. I soon learn that this is because the chicks hatch with a lot of yolk in their belly, which increases their hatch weight. They then use up this yolk, their mum's only meal ever provided.

One of our results on egg incubation is particularly baffling: the eggs are not incubated for around 20 days like in chickens and many birds, but about 60 days on average. We can estimate the approximate incubation period by labelling the shells and then finding the labelled shell fragments from hatched eggs. The volcano incubates most of them for between 50 and 80 days. For one egg incubated at relatively low temperatures, the period till hatching even lasts for 90 days! That is a long time in the soil before the chick emerges, and I wonder how the eggs avoid getting mouldy and how the embryo chicks avoid suffocating down there. These would be good topics to study in a university lab if I get the chance one day.

Photos

These photos were all taken by myself during this expedition to Tonga, between 1991 and 1993. They showcase the adventures described here. To reduce printing costs and the price of this book, they are not printed in colour. For the colour version please head to **https://anngothauthor.com/tonga/** or scan the QR code below.

Please note: The photos were taken with a manual camera as slides, long before digital cameras became available. Slides were scanned and digitally enhanced, but the quality still does not match that of today's digital cameras.

Please scan to view coloured photos

An aerial view of the volcanic island Niuafo'ou (Tin Can Island). The smaller islet on the far left is Motu Molemole, where we often camped during the week.

An aerial view of the village Esia on Niuafo'ou, including the runway for the airport.

The Moana, our first transport vessel to Niuafo'ou, is anchored safely near the volcanic shore of Niuafo'ou, with a small dinghy transporting people and luggage ashore.

The dinghy with our equipment is about to land on the only platform on Niuafo'ou. One of the women is wearing a traditional ta'ovala around her waist.

Our newly built hut awaited us on Niuafo'ou, constructed entirely from wood and woven coconut palm leaves.

Our host family dressed up for church on Sundays.

The interior of the hut which was our home for 17 months.

Malohi's outdoor kitchen, where his wife Emeni prepared most of our meals. It consisted of a firepit and a bench to keep some of the food out of reach of pigs and dogs.

The author fetching coconuts for drinking.

Walking on the only road that circumnavigates the island.

A typical village scene on Niuafo'ou, where each family clan borders their property with walls of black lava stones.

Coconut palms line the outer rim of the crater. The name Niuafo'ou translates to 'New Coconut Land.

The steep inner crater walls where the Polynesian Megapode (Malau) lived.

Barren lava fields stretch near the shore, remnants of the last volcanic eruption in 1946.

The author, hot and sweaty from the hike to Motu Molemole (the first islet visible in the background), prepares to descend the steep path from the crater rim to the lake below.

The author and a local horse taking an inflatable boat to the crater lake.

Our camp on the shore of the crater lake is equipped with solar panels to charge batteries and power a single light during the 12-hour tropical nights.

Locals preparing for a Christmas feast, with food spread out on banana leaves on the floor.

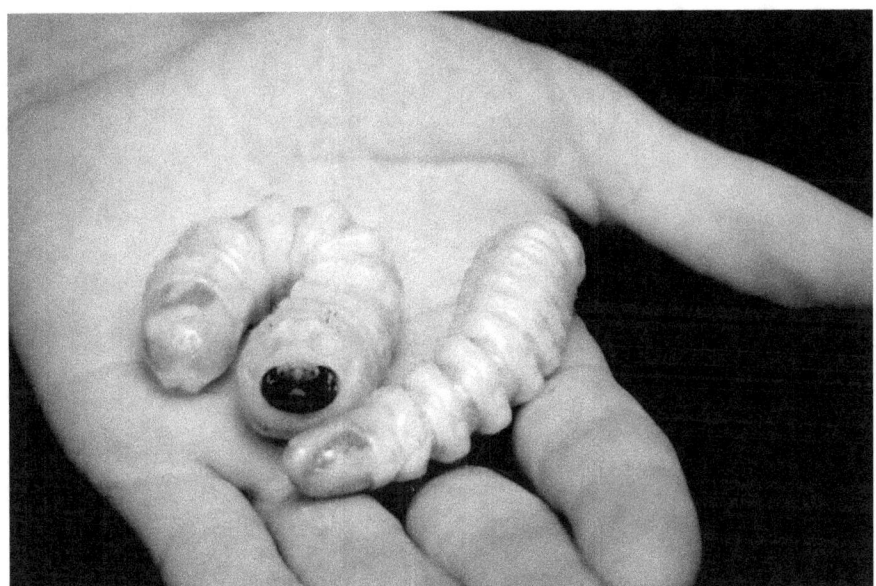
Ofato beetle larvae, a local delicacy, are usually eaten alive.

Breadfruit and shearwater, all cooked over an open fire—another local delicacy.

Malau eggs: They are incubated for up to 90 days and the shell becomes thinner as the developing chick absorbs calcium from the shell into its bones.

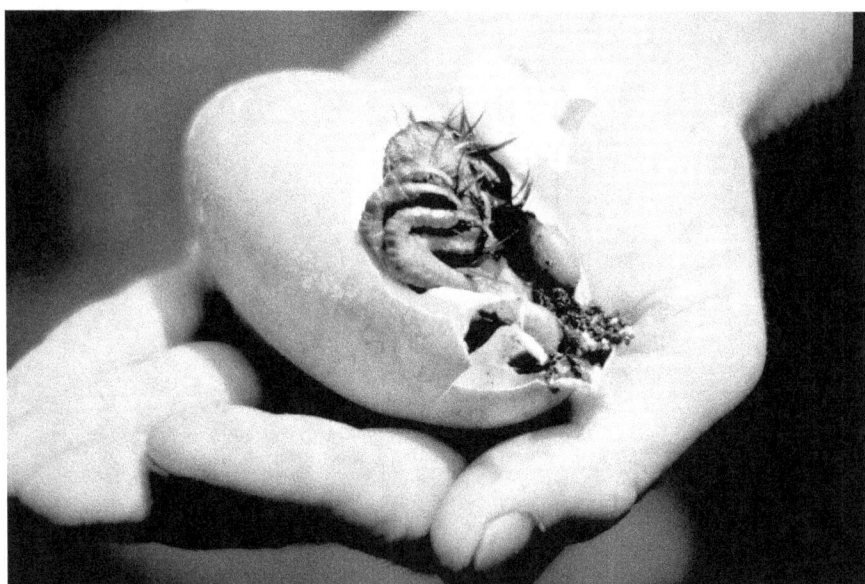

A Malau chick hatching—this one from our artificial incubator, though they typically hatch in soil as deep as 1.7 meters.

A female Malau at the entrance to an egg-laying burrow, ready to dig a nesting chamber where she will lay her egg and leave the incubation to the natural heat of the volcano.

A one-day-old Polynesian megapode chick (Malau).

The inner crater of Tofua Island, featuring a smaller, still-active volcano within the extinct larger volcano, which continues to smoke and emit sulphurous gases.

A close-up of the smaller still-active volcano on Tofua with the crater lake in the background.

Our helpers are carrying our equipment down into the inner crater of Tofua Island.

The author digging holes on Tofua, with the smoking volcano in the background. No suitable temperatures were found, making the island unsuitable for the translocation of the Malau.

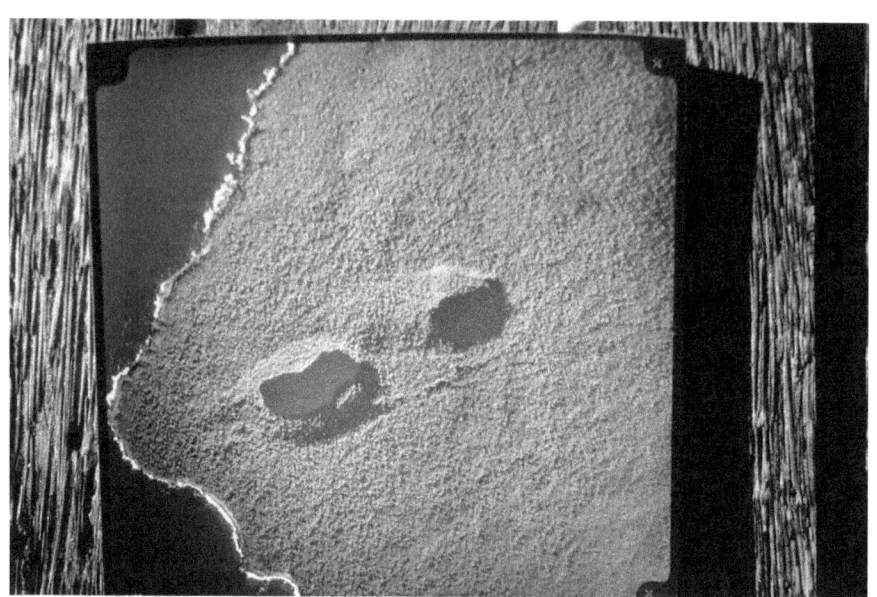

Aerial view of parts of Late Island, highlighting the small crater lake near the site where we buried Malau eggs for translocation.

Salesi and his crew were ready for the trip to Late, but with our group and equipment onboard, the boat felt overcrowded.

Landing on Late's rough shore, Salesi received some of our equipment from Vaha, who had swum it ashore through the surf, his head still visible bobbing in the sea.

16

Ivo, The Celebrity from the Air

We now seriously question whether we should stay the full two years as planned or cut our expedition shorter. The main reasons are the disagreements between the Professor and Mr Hopps. In his latest letter to us, Hopps has threatened to withdraw all his help if we don't catch birds for his zoo and follow his plans for translocating the Malau to another island.

I need to explain why we are so disillusioned. Our translocation aim is to establish a second population of Malau on another uninhabited volcanic island as a safeguard for the future. It would help this species survive if, on Niuafo'ou, the volcano were to erupt, predatory rats were to arrive, or the locals were to dig up too many eggs. To us, it is a no-brainer that we should check out other potential islands for their suitability first. They might be volcanic, but the birds may not be able to access the correct temperatures for incubation. We also need to ensure that they have similar dense vegetation to Niuafo'ou, as the Malau may not adapt to living in more open areas. Mr Hopps, on the other hand, does not want to check out the potential island and intends to translocate the birds there straight away, hoping that they will survive. Given the small remaining population of these endangered birds, we do not think it is ethical to remove individuals that may not make it through such an experiment.

Two volcanoes, in particular, seem most likely to fit the Malau's needs: Tofua and Late, both in the Vava'u island group south of us. Tofua still has an active vent inside its large caldera, so it is volcanically active. On Late Island, smoke emerged from the centre crater as late as 1854, so there might also be some 'cooking' going on underground. Both islands feature a crater lake near which warm soil for incubation is most likely to be found and large areas of broad-leafed forest similar to Niuafo'ou. Mr Hopps himself, in two of his publications, recommended Late after he visited the island. He wrote, "I have proposed this island as a potential megapode reserve, and it certainly complies with all requirements."

Now, out of the blue, Mr Hopps has changed his mind and is adamant that we need to translocate the Malau to another island called Fonualei. In Nuku'alofa, we have viewed aerial pictures of this volcano, and they have shown us that it is much smaller overall and contains little mature forest. On top of that, it has been recently active, with a lava flow produced probably during the 1980s. Volcanologists suggest that Fonualei is more likely to erupt soon than Late or Tofua[1]. Our predecessor David Todd supported our view on this island after visiting Fonualei and declared it unsuitable for a translocation because it lacks mature, broad-leafed forest[2]. Mr Hopps is well aware of this, even citing Todd's remark in one of his publications, but now chooses Fonualei nevertheless.

We don't know his exact reasons but we do have a guess. Landing a boat is easier on Fonualei than on the other volcanoes due to the presence of a small sandy beach, whereas the other islands have a perilous rocky shore. Mr Hopps expects an expensive yacht to arrive from overseas, which he will use for the translocation, and landing on Fonualei with a yacht is safer than on Late or Tofua. Fonualei also lies closer to Niuafo'ou than these two islands, so the travel time will be shorter. These are valid arguments, but they do not outweigh the disadvantages of this volcano for the Malau with its small size, risk of volcanic eruption, and lack of mature forest.

Mr Hopps also disagrees with the Professor and us that eggs should be used for the translocation instead of adult or young Malau. We are choosing eggs for two reasons. First, it is unknown whether the young chicks, when they first come out of the soil, imprint on the location where they hatched—similar to turtle hatchlings later returning to the beach where they hatched. This imprinting would mean they remember the burrow or area where they left the egg and then return to it for egg-laying later on. There is thus a

---

1. Paul Taylor, personal communication

2. Todd, D. (1983). Pritchard's Megapode on Niuafo'ou Island, Kingdom of Tonga. *Journal of the World Pheasant Association*, 8: 69-88.

chance they may not be able to find an egg-laying burrow if they are translocated as adults to an unknown island. Second, it is too risky to remove a large number of adults from a population that is already small. There are more eggs than adults, and if the translocation goes wrong, the damage to the population would be more negligible if eggs rather than adults were taken. Mr Hopps, however, is adamant that he wants to take chicks and adults. Taking eggs requires more equipment, such as an artificial incubator, which we brought from Germany. It also involves digging an egg-laying burrow in suitable temperatures on the new island home.

Summing up all these issues, Ivo and I agree that we can't remain in Tonga for the two years we had planned to stay. Instead, our new plan is to stay for one year, complete our work on Niuafo'ou, and try to check out the volcanoes Late or Tofua, or both, for their suitability as translocation islands in the future. Someone else can then discuss with Mr Hopps the best way forward and use our data to inform that decision. In a long letter to the Professor, we explain our decision, assuming he will understand. But his reply, three weeks later, is not the approval and understanding we had naively expected. On the contrary, he is annoyed with us, as he fears his reputation in front of the sponsors will suffer. In addition, he has recently published articles in German newspapers claiming that we have already initiated the translocation and that this will likely be successful. So he wants us to stay for the whole two years and carry out the translocation. We feel somewhat depressed that he is already promoting the success of this project before it has even started.

Poor Ivo has many sleepless nights before he shares his thoughts with me: He still needs to complete his studies and thesis with the Professor as his supervisor. And he won't have the energy or funds to change his supervisor or university at this late stage of his studies. On the other hand, I do not depend on the Professor because I am studying in Austria at a different university. Ivo thinks that if he leaves earlier, the Professor will no longer supervise him, and his plans for the future will go down the drain. Hence, he needs to stay for the two years we initially agreed, but he doesn't think that it is good or safe for me to continue for that long under these conditions. Hot and cold flushes conquer my body when he suggests I should go home earlier, and my emotions boil over. It doesn't take me long to decide that I, too, will stay, as I don't want to leave him alone. We both cry tears of love and frustration because our desire and enthusiasm to work in conservation are impeded by people who are supposed to supervise and support us.

One event a few days later takes our minds off the problems with the supervisors. It creates a story that the locals will likely talk about for years to come, a story that raises Ivo's status to something like a celebrity from the air. It all starts with an unusual noise approaching the island from the sea. We can't make out what it is until we see a small seaplane approaching. If there were Fata Morganas in the South Pacific, this would be one.

The plane lands on the lake near our camp, and a middle-aged guy named Werner steps out. He lives on the island of Vava'u further south, where he owns a diving business and a seaplane. Occasionally, he earns extra money from the Tongan government by checking out Tonga's border islands with his aircraft. Never before have we crossed the lake that quickly, and soon we join him in his plane, where he shares his steak, cheese, and salad with us. Heavenly food that, right now, tastes as if it is from another world. Werner, originally from Austria, is equally surprised to run into us as we are to meet him, and it feels rather good to talk to a pālangi, even in our own language, to feel admired for what we do, and to get some news from the outside world from him.

After some chatting, Werner even offers a sightseeing tour of the island with a stopover in Esia, but the plane can only carry one passenger. This person has to be Ivo, as it would cause turmoil if I, as a woman, were to arrive by plane in Esia with a man who is not my husband. The two men first circle the island, much to Ivo's delight, then land on Esia's grass strip. Soon the whole village knows and runs to the airport. The locals are torn between heralding Ivo's arrival from the air like a surprise from heaven or a work of the *tevolo*. The last time Malohi saw Ivo, he was walking off to the lake with me, and now he arrives on a plane with a stranger. The locals obviously haven't heard the seaplane coming from the West, and their surprise at its appearance couldn't be topped by much. They crowd around Ivo and treat him like a celebrity, and he needs to explain to Malohi repeatedly why he has arrived like this. Malohi asks him to confirm many times that he will not leave the island with the plane but will return to me on Motu Molemole afterwards. Poor Malohi keeps shaking his head; this is almost too much to understand, and his face speaks more than words when Ivo says goodbye with the phrase, "I am flying back to the lake now!" At the lake, Werner kindly hands over three National Geographic magazines he brought with him. We trust him with the letters to our parents, and he heads off, back to Vava'u. We drop everything, even forgetting to cook dinner, and we read every line in those magazines twice, like addicts who have received a new supply of drugs. My brain starts spinning from sudden stimulation: talking to another pālangi and reading magazines from the outside world!

17

The Professor and War Day Arrive

Our plans to fly to the main island, Tongatapu, for visa and shopping purposes have been disrupted by the Professor, who has decided to visit us earlier than planned, in the second week of November 1991. He has already arrived in Nuku'alofa and somehow, with his assertive manner, has managed to get an audience with His Excellency, the King of Tonga, Tāufa'āhau Tupou IV. The latter has been king since 1965 and is one of the longest-reigning monarchs in the world. We are more than relieved and grateful when we receive a telegram from the Professor in which he informs us that his audience has solved our visa issues: the King has promised a research visa.

While waiting for his flight in Nuku'alofa, the Professor has also organised a rubber dinghy, including an outboard engine, that will make our trip along the crater lake more feasible. He has also discovered that it is possible to send a telegram to Niuafo'ou, which we didn't know. In his telegram to us, the Professor has asked that we call him in his hotel, and we do as requested. This call involves another trip to the social telephone hub on the island, Laveni and a few other local ladies in tow, and another disappointed crowd when I talk to the Professor in German rather than English or Tongan. He tells me the exciting news that a ship full of supplies is finally due to arrive, around the same time as himself.

And even better: he offers to send some essential supplies with the ship, together with the dinghy and outboard engine.

The exact arrival time of the ship is unknown and has so far only been narrowed down to a 10-day timeframe. One would think that someone on this island, or on Tongatapu, could find out, but instead, people accept that the ship will come in Tongan Time. Interestingly, the Tongan language here includes three different expressions for events in the future: in a while, in a little while, and in a long while. We are given one of these three answers, in apparently random order, whenever we ask about the ship's arrival time.

The ship's imminent arrival has introduced an inevitable sense of anticipation and a rush of activities in the village. The ladies sweep the floors more often, smack their kids and dogs more frequently, and sit together outside for hours to talk about all that flour, salt, and sugar they are hoping to obtain from the ship. Likewise, the men pace up and down, hoping the tobacco delivery won't be too far away.

We, too, are excited, hoping that our new supplies, dinghy, and outboard engine won't get damaged or lost on the trip. Kailao tells us that one can even get ice cream and chocolate on the ship. While we pretend that these earthly goods are not essential to us, there is a fine line between joking and seriously craving them. Such cravings also extend to news from the outside world—we listen to German radio whenever our solar panels have charged our batteries. Unfortunately, we have run out of novels to read and recently realised that we have started reading aloud the labels on our corned beef and sardine tins repeatedly, not to mention how often we have read those National Geographic magazines by now. That is how desperate we are for reading material. We really would appreciate a bit more mental distraction at times.

While the anticipation in the village increases by the minute, Ivo suddenly suffers from a high fever, for unknown reasons. He cannot move, sleeps sweaty under our mosquito net, and his illness leaves me both worried and in charge of unloading our goods from the ship. I try to find out when the vessel might arrive but can't find Malohi, and when I question his wife Emeni, she replies, *"apongipongi pongipong."* I think this means 'tomorrow morning', but I am not sure, and I am worried that our supplies will never be unloaded.

The following day, Kailao comes by and confirms that the boat has arrived before dawn, at 4 am and that Malohi and most other men have slept at Futu, near the rocky landing platform that constitutes our 'harbour', in the hope of getting to the supplies and tobacco first. We offer our last packet of tobacco to Kailao in return for his help with bringing back our dinghy, engine, and supplies. Kailao kindly does so, and when he returns after some hours, we are pleased to see that the Professor has sent some of the things we requested. At least we are now better equipped for the next few weeks. We both feel glad when Ivo's fever disappears the next day, but he is disappointed that he missed out on the chocolate and ice cream on the ship. I didn't dare include chocolate among the essentials that I had asked the Professor to send.

The day after the ship's arrival is 'war day', as Kailao calls it. It is the day when the local shop, usually empty, finally sells a few goods. When we arrive at the little shed made of corrugated iron, the shop's shelves appear relatively sparsely filled. Many items don't ever seem to make it to the shop because relatives of the shop owner insist on the local custom of sharing everything you have. We hope to fill our plastic buckets with sugar and flour. When I first ask the shop owner for 4 kg of flour, he refuses to give me any at all, and through this gesture, he makes it clear that there is a cap on how much you are allowed to buy. As I walk out the door, he calls after me and offers 3 kg, and I am allowed to add that to the bit of sugar, soya oil, and matches I have already managed to gather. My biggest treats, though, are one tin of Milo hot chocolate powder and one packet of Arnott's arrowroot cookies that I proudly present to Ivo upon my return. These treasures can be a small consolation for the missed treats on the ship and for not having bought any chocolate during that last rushed shopping trip in Nuku'alofa months ago.

The Professor's initial arrival date by plane has already been delayed twice. First, because of a cyclone that lingered in the area. Lucky for us, it passed Tonga but unfortunately then caused havoc on nearby Tuvalu Island. The second time, the flight was cancelled because of some technical defect in the Twin Otter machine. With all these delays, our parents haven't received any mail for a while and must be worried, so we have decided to send them a telegram. The operator who looks after the one and only phone is also the official who can assist with that. "No problem," he says when we ask to send a telegram to Germany. We noticed before that when Tongans are not so sure about things or don't know how to do them at all, they maintain a very proud and calm demeanour. The operator is very calm and shows no sign of nervousness. He spends a while looking through a list of countries on a mouldy piece of paper to find the prefix number for Germany and how much it would cost, and he then asks, "Telegram for West Germany or East Germany?" Never mind that the two countries united almost two years ago, and East Germany no longer exists. The paperwork on this island hasn't caught up with that news. We settle on West Germany and manage to send off the short don't-worry message to our parents.

Eventually, the Professor arrives, not just like an ordinary passenger on a plane, but as a kind of celebrity whose arrival is observed by about 300 islanders who have gathered around the 'airport'. His celebrity status is caused by the fact that he has somehow convinced the German manager of Royal Tongan Airline to fly to Niuafo'ou on a Sunday because he didn't want to wait any longer. That has never been heard of before—planes are not supposed to arrive on a Sunday, the holy day dedicated to church-going. The Professor is a man who is used to getting his way, and with his 1.9 m stature and king-like demeanour, he impresses people quite easily. Ivo, in contrast, is only 1.6 m tall and struggles to be accepted just because of this short, lean stature. When the Professor steps out of the plane on a Sunday, wearing an expedition vest with lots of filled pockets, people stare at him as if he were an alien straight from space. It appears some locals have even skipped one of the two or three daily church visits to be part of this spectacle.

We have arranged for the Professor to live in the house attached to the police station, as it constitutes the best accommodation available in Esia. It is built from lava stone and concrete, and it has genuine windows and doors that can even be locked. Also, no inmate currently occupies the jail as no pigs or barbed fencing wire have been stolen, and no homebrew alcohol has been produced. Our arrangement required careful negotiation with Malohi, who was initially very offended by the idea that Kailao and not he should host this new guest. Eventually, Malohi agreed, still a bit miffed at being side-tracked. For the men here, maintaining their social status is very important. Malohi probably thinks his status might suffer by not accommodating the Professor, even if he doesn't have a suitable room.

While we are thankful to the Professor for sorting out our visa issues and organising some supplies, we struggle with his attitude towards the locals in the weeks to come. He does not attempt to understand their culture but rather orders them around like a colonialist would have done with natives decades ago. This behaviour leads to limited success as the locals are proud and ignore him when it's too much for them. Our proud guide, Lakepi, in particular, is highly amused by the Professor's requests. For example, the Professor is determined to help us improve our trap design and, on one of our excursions to the bush, asks Lakepi to show him how he builds the traps for catching Malau. Lakepi starts doing so right then and there, where the Professor has asked him, but then the Professor wants him to do it in a different location, indicating that place in a bossy manner. Lakepi thinks this is silly and heads home, without building traps or fetching the coconuts we need to drink that day.

We also have a private word with Kailao, who is quite stressed about hosting his guest. The Professor asked him to fix a door for him on a Sunday, the no-work day, and Kailao is clearly not allowed to do that. On top of that, the Professor also expects fresh meat for dinner every day. One day, we watch Kailao head off with his rifle to try to shoot a stray chicken in the bush, which is a desperate measure as they are rare and hard to find. We quietly call him over to tell him that the Professor can eat what we eat and live as we live. This means only breadfruit and coconut on some days at least. The more the Professor finds out how we survive here, the better he will understand.

Initially, we struggle to convey to the Professor why our studies on the Malau are progressing rather slowly. He doesn't seem to grasp why we are spending so much time obtaining and preparing food and drinking water, fighting the humidity, and carefully maintaining our fragile bonds with the locals. He slowly starts to understand some of this over the next two weeks, at least the bit about humidity and food. We show him some of our equipment falling apart in the humid climate, despite our attempts to keep it moisture-free with silica gel every night. Ivo's leather belt is so mouldy that it crumbles in his hands, and our fuel stove, torch, and stopwatch are close to dying. Some of this equipment is essential for our work, and if it fails, we can't get a replacement.

While the Professor is starting to understand our situation better, his attitude towards the locals doesn't change. One day, he gives Lakepi one, only one, piece of cigarette paper. However, he first demands that Lakepi ask him like a beggar, and then he wants him to say thank you gratefully several times. Afterwards, he eats a whole tin of corned beef in front of our local guide while offering him a piece of his breadfruit. Corned beef is like gold to these people, breadfruit like mud. We hate watching this, as we know how proud Lakepi is, how much he needs cigarette paper and cherishes corned beef, and how much he must despise the Professor for this treatment.

We are concerned that the Professor might seriously damage the locals' attitude towards us pālangi in general, and are glad when he leaves after two weeks on Tin Can Island. He plans to visit another research station in the Philippines on the way home and asks us to give him half of our bottle of iodine disinfectant in case he might get a wound there. Professor or not, we have to decline, as we are supposed to stay on this island for another year or more, and injuries can become infected quickly and badly in this climate. This minor incident shows us how selfish the Professor is in many ways and how we are mainly here to help him sell his big conservation success to a broad audience upon his return.

18

Critters in Oats and an Ear

The Professor has left, and it is time to do more work. While Motu Molemole has become like our second home, we also need to explore the Malau nesting grounds in other parts of the island, especially around the southern shore of the crater lake. The smaller secondary lake where we set up camp is called Vai Si'i, meaning "small water," compared to the large crater lake Vai Lahi. Unfortunately, our equipment in this temporary base is too tempting for the locals, who seem to frequently pass by and admire all the things we have—equipment and corned beef that they can only dream of. Kailao has advised us always to lock up everything, but that's too hard when camping. We can't lock our tent, and most equipment is easy to carry away. As a result, one of us has to constantly guard the camp and chat with the locals who pass by, while the other studies the Malau. The one advantage of being visited more often, especially by young men, is that we can ask them to retrieve the drinking coconuts from the high palm trees for us. Of course, they are happy to do that—in return for some cigarette paper.

The person on camp duty is busy with the everyday chores that this climate requires. Making a fire for cooking is starting to become a point of contention between us, as whoever is on fire duty needs to find dry wood to burn. I have carefully stacked away a small pile under our water tarp, but Ivo has not, and it seems to me that he is occasionally helping himself to my dry wood or even using our limited supply of kerosene to start the fire. Perhaps there is a little bit of a pyromaniac in him as his face lights up as soon as the kerosene turns into a flame, but perhaps the lack of other entertainment makes this everyday chore so much fun. I have to ask him to stop that amusement, though, as kerosene is essential for lighting our fuel stove when cooking oats with milk powder for breakfast. Theoretically, we could eat the oats raw, but beetles have invaded them. The only way to get rid of the critters is to cook the oats in hot water, which causes the beetles to die and float on the water's surface. We then fish those out with a spoon and consume the oats with only the occasional beetle in them.

Our little arguments over firewood aside, we are getting on excellently, and after dark at 5 pm, we both agree it is worth using a bit of wood to burn a fire next to which we can just sit around while chatting and listening to the noises around us. Sometimes, when we have enough sun to charge our batteries with the solar panels, we can listen to whatever we receive on our world receiver radio. There is not much else to do. The tropical nights last about 12 hours, and we can't sleep that long. Whenever we feel a bit bored or exhausted, we remind each other of the many great aspects of our expedition, such as the unique cultural insights, our progress with studying a bird that is little known, the absence of a cold winter, and the intense short sunsets over the crater lake.

Our work with the Malau is now made easier by the dinghy, which transports us along the shores of the steep, dense forests of the inner crater rim. This way, we can reach hidden egg-laying grounds and count the birds using a method in which we play their calls from our Walkman recorder and then count how many respond. These trips are such a luxury, and we enjoy the incredible vistas from the boat of lush green forests, fascinating lava rock formations, and emerald green bays of the lake. More and more puzzle pieces fit into our overall picture of the Malau, and all of these will help us develop a conservation plan for this species.

As part of our conservation mission, we first write down and distribute some simple messages for the local people, which we use to educate them about the main threats to the Malau and the importance of conserving this species for the future. Second, we are now more serious about planning to visit another volcanic island, either Tofua or Late, and inspect it as a potential translocation island for the Malau. Royal Tongan Airways promises to connect our island to Vava'u soon after Christmas, so this may be feasible. However, travelling to Tofua or Late from Vava'u will still be an adventure, as they are both quite remote and uninhabited.

Before this, though, we spend Christmas and a few more weeks on Niuafo'ou. Apart from intense studies of the birds, we use this opportunity to visit the more remote villages near the south coast. Villagers in these last dwellings on the island road have seen pālangis less often and don't ask for tobacco or corned beef as much, even though they seem poorer. Their houses are traditional, made from woven coconut leaves instead of corrugated iron, concrete, or other expensive building materials. The people here also speak little English, and the children are scared of us. Our attempts to converse in Tongan are well received, and we are given some bananas, pineapples, and sugar cane as presents.

In return for their gifts, several families ask us to take photos of them, not now, but next Sunday, when everyone will have dressed up for church. We are more than happy to return to the villages for the photo sessions and are again surprised by the nice clothes these people own, even if they don't have much else. The men and boys wear sparkling white shirts, the ladies and girls wear colourful dresses, and all are decorated with their best ta'ovalas. They don't often get a photo taken, and they will surely treasure this one and maybe send it to their relatives overseas.

Back in Esia, a nasty shock overshadows one of the coming nights for Ivo. He wakes up screaming in pain, and I can barely understand his urgent requests for a bucket full of water. He dunks his head underwater as often as he can to flush his right ear because an insect of some sort has started exploring his eardrum while he has been asleep. This is causing him excruciating pain. All our neighbours come running to see what's happening while Ivo keeps screaming and flushing his ear. It takes quite a while for the stupid critter to stop crawling and for one of our potent painkillers to work. Now we can only hope that we won't need the attention of the island's medical officer and that any irritation caused by the critter exploring his eardrum will disappear by itself. It is reassuring to know that we have some antibiotics in our first aid kit, should he need them. From now on, we decide, we will always sleep with cotton wool stuck in our ears. This has the additional advantage that we won't hear the church bells at 4:30 am as loudly as before.

19

Christmas and New Year

We have completed our studies on the south coast and have returned to Esia for Christmas. On Christmas Eve, we are flabbergasted by a discovery: the locals can bake bread! Lakepi invites us to his house and presents us with an actual crusty loaf of white bread, which smells and tastes like the best thing we have ever tasted. He has baked it in an old oil drum in which he has made a fire and somehow positioned the tin with dough above it. Even more astonishingly, he pulls out a tin of butter to have with it. I never knew you could buy butter preserved in a tin that lasts for months, and somehow, he must have stored this prized possession somewhere, tucked away for Christmas. We can only guess why bread is not made more often during the year: breadfruit is easier to get, and yeast, if available at all, is used for other, more critical alcoholic concoctions.

We hand out corned beef, tinned peas and cigarette paper to Lakepi and his family but keep some for Kailao, who has also invited us to his house. He and his wife even own a plastic Christmas tree decorated with balloons, tinsel, and lollies. After a shared meal and lots of laughter, Kailao also presents us with a loaf of bread in return. We feel like we are in heaven.

On Christmas Eve, every family celebrates with food and song throughout most of the night. After church the next day, families gift each other with bread and cakes, and most people, including us, get together in the village for one big feast. Food is presented on banana leaves and mats on the floor, while people sit around this centrepiece, in an order determined by their social status. Laveni has just arrived with a pile of Tapa fabrics in her arms, which are presents for others. People here value these fabrics highly and often give them as gifts, especially at weddings and Christmas, with the women spend many days creating them. They first collect the inner bark of the paper mulberry tree (*Broussonetia papyrifera*), then soak it before beating it for hours into a thin fabric with a wooden mallet. Once dry, they decorate it with beautiful patterns in black and rust-brown colours. In Esia, the continuous 'thonk' sound of women beating the Tapa often adds to all the other background noises of village life.

What strikes us is the strict rules that guide this Christmas festivity. It is not just a random get-together where people chat, not a party as we would attend at home. Random chatting is not allowed. Instead, every adult participant seems to have a designated role in this society, and people are quite serious and determined to fit into that role. Many speeches are held, food is passed around, and we practise our cross-legged sitting while missing the impulsiveness of festivities at home. Kailao later explains that a person's position in this society is determined by age, gender and ancestors, i.e., their line of descent. Luckily, women are highly regarded, and a 15-year-old girl has a higher social status than her 20-year-old brother.

Laveni, our host's daughter, sits next to me and identifies the chunks of meat for us: local pork, a bit of imported beef, and more pork. Next to her sits a young woman, about Laveni's age, with rather masculine features—a wide jaw with a prominent chin, thick bushy eyebrows, and a broad nose. Her chest is also rather flat. I throw some careful side glances at her, but she must be a woman as Laveni is allowed to talk to her. She wouldn't at all be allowed to speak to a young man. On the way home, Laveni solves the mystery. With a giggle, she asks, "You see that girl? She is a boy." She then adds, "Her mum says she is a girl so she can help with cooking." I now remember a paragraph in our book about Tongan culture. It describes the custom of fakaleiti, which is raising a boy as a girl. If a Tongan woman has too many sons and needs someone to help her with the cooking and other chores, she can bring up one of the sons as a daughter. The girl-boy mixes easily with the rest of the family, and nobody raises an eyebrow about her/him.

After a long lunch rest, people gather around the local band. Their clothes are now less formal, more colourful, and some have exchanged the formal ta'ovala waist mats for a waistband of woven strips of pandanus, called kiekie. The local musicians' band consists of seven young men who sing while making music with four instruments: guitars, ukuleles, two old pieces of metal as percussion instruments, and a fourth homemade string instrument. The latter is made out of one wooden board from which another wooden pole sticks out vertically. The player creates a deep-sounding bass sound by plucking the one string that is attached to the end of the board on one side and the end of the pole on the other side. This creative music finally resembles the type of festivity we enjoy, less serious and more like the lively and vibrant South Pacific we have envisaged.

With Christmas behind us, we venture back to Motu Molemole, only to be disturbed by four teenage boys who come swimming across with their pack of dogs. They have come to hunt the remaining goats that still live on this islet. Uttering something like war cries, they disappear into the bush, only to return with a different prey than a goat: a dead Malau, wrapped around the head of one of the boys like a scarf, with its legs tied to its beak. We are shocked, of course, but try not to show it. They are testing us, demonstrating that we have nothing to say on this islet, and they are not interested in us trying to tell them about endangered birds. So we ignore their head decoration and stay near them, pretending to do our work while they linger around for another hour, smoking, chatting, and drinking coconuts. Later, we tell Kailao about this sad incident and hope that he will find a way to stop such visits and maybe even such meaningless killing of an endangered species.

We mark New Year's Eve with our last packet of cookies and draw happy pigs onto each other's bellies. What else can you do on an islet on the island so far away from fireworks and champagne? So the year 1992 starts like all our other days on Motu Molemole: an early rise, off to the hide near the laying ground, observing the Malau and taking notes. This time, though, we hear many more voices from people around the crater lake, some of them shouting out to us. An algal bloom has turned the lake quite green, which seems to promote the reproduction of the Tilapia fish. Compared to fish caught in the sea, they are tiny, but the local men now gather in large groups around the lake every day to catch the fish. They spend hours before they collect enough to make a meal, and they eat most of them straight away, directly out of the fire. This doesn't seem a very efficient way of obtaining food, especially as it doesn't provide much for the women and children waiting back home. Fishing in the sea would yield much more but is not as pleasant, especially if the surf pounds against the lava rocks. We recently gave Kailao all our larger fishing hooks to fish from the ocean shore. A week later, when we asked him why he spent all day fishing for small Tilapia in the lake instead, he claimed not to have any hooks for fishing in the sea.

On our last return trip to Esia, we have to carry quite a bit of gear, as our departure for Vava'u is approaching, and we don't want to leave any valuables on Motu Molemole. Luckily, Malohi passes by on the island road, so we get a lift on the trailer of his tractor and a chance to feel like locals. He and his men have been fishing and collecting essentials for the Sunday feast. Every square centimetre of the trailer is covered in either firewood, banana leaves, young or old coconuts, as well as baskets containing fresh fish or root vegetables. The men push aside some of the load to place our barrels in between, which we gratefully accept as seats, while the five men sit, like fakirs, cross-legged on a pile of coconuts, stoically and without any movement during the whole bumpy ride. A little later, we stop to take on more fishers with their 10-metre-long bamboo stick that they have used as a fishing rod and more fish. Malohi's improvised bus seems full to us. Still, nobody is left behind, and he also takes on a few teenagers who are walking along the village road with a bundle of cooking bananas and the long sticks they have used to hunt shearwaters. At home, I would probably feel shy sitting jammed in between so many men and their gear, but here it just feels good. I never notice any inappropriate looks. Instead, the men are courteous, passing me, in particular, young coconuts to drink and keeping away the many overhanging branches that threaten to hit us in the face. Our short dialogues in Tongan about Ofato and other important topics are received with warm smiles. We are happy because, at this very moment, we feel like we are just one of them and not just pālangis who stand outside their culture all the time.

20

Vava'u and Tofua Volcano

It is early February 1992, and we are due to leave for Vava'u and Tofua tomorrow. In our book about Tongan culture, we read that "Hosts may give gifts to the honoured or new guests when they leave. It is an extreme insult to decline such offers, which may include food, handicrafts, fruit, or tapa cloth." We do not think of this information when visiting Laione on the day before our planned departure to Vava'u. All we want is to say goodbye and have a friendly chat, but Laione insists on slaughtering a piglet for us and fetching his best taro and yams from his plantation. We are given the—in his eyes—best bits of the meat, such as the fatty blubber and skin. Our kind host family waits until we have finished our meal before they start eating. Kailao also happens to pass by, accidentally or not, and joins in the feast and happy conversations. Of course, we ask what Laione would like us to bring from Vava'u in return, and he mentions a large torch, so he doesn't have to fear the *tevolo*—the devil—at night. Naturally, we will also need to supply him with lots of batteries, as he won't get those here either. Kailao mentions that he would 'only' like two rolls of barbed wire to fence his plantation.

Our flight the next day leaves at 11 am. At 9 am, we are all packed and ready to go, full from our last few oats for breakfast. Naively, we haven't considered that Malohi would also follow the tradition. He serves a freshly roasted piglet with manioc and yams for breakfast. Knowing how valuable this meal is for him, we thank him many times and retreat to our hut for the time it usually takes to eat and appreciate this present. We really can't eat much of this well-meant rich meal so soon after our breakfast and yesterday's fatty feast, but we also can't offend him. We secretly pack some pork in our luggage for Vava'u, together with Malohi's wish list of things to bring back: towels, tobacco, thongs, glass cylinders for petroleum lamps, flour, vegetable seeds, marbles for the kids, and a few other items.

The pig feast causes us to rush to the airport—the first time in months that we have to hurry like this. We should have guessed that the plane would be two hours late anyway, as hardly anything leaves on time in Tonga—Tongan Time! Before we finally board, all passengers are weighed on a large scale with a big display, a scale usually used to weigh the luggage. The capacity of the small Twin Otter plane is not determined by the number of passengers but by the mass it can carry without falling out of the sky. Most adult Tongans are well-rounded, and being 'big fat' is a status symbol. This means only every second seat on the plane can be filled, and the pilot comes around to hand out extension parts for the seatbelts. We definitely don't need those as we have lost weight during these last few months and have to buy some urgently needed new trousers in Vava'u.

Our 1.5-hour flight to Neiafu, the capital of Vava'u, is marked by four strong feelings. First, the amazing feeling of sitting on a soft seat instead of cross-legged on the floor. Second, the torture of watching the pilot eat a sandwich on multigrain bread in front of our eyes, followed by the sensation of shrivelling in the air-conditioned dry air after having lived in 80% humidity for months. Feeling number four is the joy that overcomes us when we see 'our' island from the air—for me, this is the first time ever. While the pilot circles it once, we spot all those places that have been so hard to reach by bush-bashing. We notice how proud we are to have visited so many areas of the island already, but there are quite a few that we have not yet seen.

Upon arrival in Vava'u, we are prevented from rushing to the shops, restaurants, hairdresser, and hotel as quickly as we had hoped. Instead, a loudspeaker announcement informs us that all the people at the small airport need to sit down on the floor. An important guest is soon to arrive on another plane, a highly significant person indeed. Tonga has three layers of social status: royal, noble, and commoner, and today's guest is at the top of the royal category: the Tongan King himself. Tonga has been a self-governing kingdom that never relinquishes its sovereignty to any foreign power for many years. The current King, his Excellency Tāufa'āhau Tupou IV, is the fourth in a long line of queens and kings that have ruled the country since 1797. Tongan etiquette requires you to sit when a person of high social position arrives, and it doesn't get any higher than that. After an hour or so of sitting around, the plane with the King finally arrives. First, the 74-year-old monarch steps from the aircraft onto decorative mats, leaning on a walking stick. Then, we are lucky enough to get a quick glimpse of him before he disappears in a Land Rover. He wears big bulky ski goggles, the German brand name UVEX written on the side strap. We know that in Tonga, wearing fancy sunglasses raises your status, and obviously, these are very fancy. Someone tells us later that they were a German guest's recent donation to his Excellency. Do we wonder whether this is how the Professor managed to get his interview with the King? He never told us.

It goes without saying how much we enjoy the comforts of Western civilisation during the days that follow. For a few days, it is goodbye to Anga Faka-Tongá, the Tongan way of life, and hello, welcome, to Anga Faka-Pālangi, the Western way. Sleeping in a real bed under a fan in our Hilltop Guesthouse, with a shower and fully loaded fruit bowl next to us, are just some of the comforts we enjoy.

There is not much time to appreciate our critter-free hotel and be lazy, though, because we learn that soon, a ship will arrive that is scheduled to travel to Niuafo'ou and then on to Samoa. This vessel is our only opportunity to gather and send up some supplies for our friends and ourselves on the island. Gathering all our supplies is like finding a needle in a haystack, but luckily we have the help of Rolf. He is an Austrian man who has built the Hilltop Guesthouse, and we have become friends. He has had a rather interesting life on different continents and is very creative in finding ways to make money in Vava'u. Apart from the Hilltop guesthouse, he also runs a shop that sells imported delicacies from Italy, and he is involved in selling real estate. His wife Lautoka, much younger than him, is Tongan, and they have a young son. Rolf asked us to teach his son some German during our stay in Neiafu. In return, he tries to help whenever he can. Assisted by his insights and connections, we manage to pack some bags with all the goods we have to send to Niuafo'ou in the limited time available.

As usual, it is impossible to find out when exactly the ship will anchor. By now, we understand the meaning when a local man advises us that the vessel will arrive "*apongipongi pongiponi*"—tomorrow morning. But the following day, we are told the next day, and that day the news is that it will be at midnight tonight. So waiting around at the harbour for two days becomes our favourite pastime until the ship finally arrives at 4 am.

The official name of this ship is *Fokololo-oe Hau*, but the locals call it a Tongan name that translates to something like a "swimming coffin". Like the *Moana*, it was initially built as a river ferry in China and then donated to Tonga. No changes were ever made to properly equip the ship for the high seas it has to traverse here. We don't envy the people who wait to board, including some on their way to Samoa. With them travel truckloads full of bananas, coconuts, root vegetables, and pigs in cages, all to be sold at markets in Samoa.

For the first time since our arrival, long after our supplies have been loaded, we witness hectic behaviour and stress in Tongans. They need to package all their goods in containers suitable for shipping, and they do so until after the ship's horn has already signalled its imminent departure. One large family arrives as the horn blows, with the back of their pickup truck full of green bananas. The older children throw the fruit to the father, and he quickly stuffs them into bags, while the grandmother creates a string from some bark and sews up the bags. Mum is busy keeping the younger children together, while another family member somehow manages to secure a container to load all the bags in. We have never seen Tongans move that fast, and somehow the family and bananas all end up on the vessel. All in Tongan Time!

Our luxury time in Vava'u has to come to an end because we need to venture closer to Tofua, the volcanic island that might be suitable for translocating the Malau. We know it has a crater lake and a small active vent inside the larger extinct crater, which seems promising for finding warm soil where we could bury Malau eggs as part of our translocation project. Tofua Island is quite remote; hence some island hopping is required to get there. Island hopping through coral islands to get to a volcanic island.

The islands in Tonga are arranged a bit like two parallel strings of beads, to the west where two tectonic plates meet. Here, at the Tonga Trench, the Pacific plate slides under the Indo-Pacific plate, and this causes materials in the descending plate to heat and rise to the surface, forming volcanoes. Tofua is one bead on the string of volcanic islands; Late, Fonualei, and our island Niuafo'ou further north are others. Sometimes new islands even appear on this string, or others disappear[1]. The beads on the eastern string are islands of different origins, formed by corals. In contrast to the volcanic islands, they are flat and mainly consist of sand and coral rubble, and their soil is less fertile than volcanic soil.

Our mission is to find a coral island on the eastern string, from which we can then battle the winds and high seas to get to Tofua Island. Lifuka, the largest coral island, is our first destination. No planes fly there, so we find a vessel that crosses the 120 km from Neiafu to Lifuka in one night. By now, we are experts in sleeping on the open deck of a ship that is more suited to carrying goods than people. Our arrival in Pangai, the largest settlement on Lifuka, is marked by fireworks in the sea. While people unload the vessel at 4 am, the sea shimmers in sparkling green colours, especially when the water gets disturbed

---

1. In 2014, a suboceanic eruption caused the appearance of a new island called Hunga Tonga—Hunga Ha'apai https://svs.gsfc.nasa.gov/12800. This volcano erupted violently causing widespread death and destruction in January 2022 *https://www.dfat.gov.au/crisis-hub/hunga-tonga-hunga-haapai-volcanic-eruption-and-tsunami*. At least another 50 volcanoes have erupted under water in much deeper depths along this chain *https://schmidtocean.org/cruise-log-post/tonga-kingdom-volcanoes/*

by boats. It looks like an explosion of glowing glitter but is caused by light-producing bioluminescent bacteria. What a sight! Our feeling of being in the tropics continues when we find accommodation in the only guest house on Lifuka. Two young Germans have established it, offering many comforts, such as a proper bed and a petroleum lamp. Outside our hut, the water laps gently against a glorious white sand beach, and in the near distance, a blue and turquoise shimmering sea and reef fringe the island.

It would be nice to stay for a holiday, but Tofua is waiting for us. Luckily, the Tongan manager of the guest house has a friend who has a brother named Afah who sometimes visits Tofua. Afah lives on Kotu, a small coral cay that is closest to Tofua Island, and our contacts alert him to our arrival. Apparently, Afah is willing to take us to Tofua for a price yet to be negotiated. So, goodbye to Western comfort, and again welcome authentic insights into Tongan culture!

Getting to Kotu is an adventure in itself. Pālangis don't usually go there, so we need to travel as Tongans do. The vessel that services this island doesn't seem to have a name; at least we can't find it. We need to board at midnight and wonder once more why most boats in Tonga seem to start or end their journey when people are supposed to sleep. But the worst part is that it stinks, really stinks, from the moment we enter. A steward tells us to deposit our luggage downstairs in the storeroom, which is already full of pigs in cages, goats tethered by ropes, baskets upon baskets full of green bananas, and much else. The smell coming from all these goods, especially the poor animals that have already travelled from other islands, is simply revolting. We spend the next seven hours at sea, sitting on some dilapidated seats in the bowels of this boat with a nauseous stomach and half-asleep before we arrive somewhere near Kotu as the sun rises.

We hear the rattling of the anchor but have no idea where exactly we are because nobody has told us that the coral reef around Kotu is so extensive that bigger vessels can't get near it without risking severe damage to their hulls. So instead, we anchor somewhere else and eventually manage to find a local who informs us that we are anchored off Ha'afeva, an island 8 km to the west. All of a sudden, hectic activity breaks out. Everyone tries to get their luggage out of the storeroom at once, and we struggle to find ours underneath goat droppings, pig excrement, and squashed bananas. It is hard to find out what is going on, especially if you don't speak fluent Tongan. We keep repeating the name of our fisherman—Afah, Afah—until several people rather vehemently push us through a small hatch into a small boat. This dinghy has a tiny space free for us and bobs up and down in a rather precarious manner. Somehow, our luggage follows with more goods and a baby that someone pushes into my arms. I can't imagine a more chaotic way of boarding a boat, or a boat fuller than that!

I'm not sure which feeling is strongest: nausea, confusion, or the stress of having to hold onto a baby, our luggage, and the rickety boat all at the same time, so early in the morning. Only the baby's smile cheers me up. It is not at all bothered by all this commotion. Like all Tongan babies, it is accustomed to lying in other people's arms. Also uplifting is a call from the helmsman, a man named Tavite, who would later become an essential part of our exploration team on Tofua Island. He yells out, "*Sai pālangi?*"—"Are you okay pālangi?"—over the heads of all the passengers on the boat. During the next hour or so, under the day's first sunlight, I start to relax, and Tavite skilfully manoeuvres the boat through the reef, sometimes only a few centimetres above the corals. The aquamarine and turquoise colours in the reef are astonishing, and we can even see details of the many colourful corals, fish, and clams beneath us. I am careful not to drop the baby while leaning overboard to watch the marine life below. As a mountain girl, I have never seen a coral reef before, only read about its immense biodiversity and beauty, and I am so fascinated by what I see!

Upon landing on Kotu, a lady takes the baby and returns it to its rightful mother, then guides us to the house of Afah. Once more, we are the only white people on a remote island, and the locals stare at us accordingly. Several kids run away upon seeing us, obviously not acquainted with white people. Our limited Tongan language skills come in handy when talking to Afah and negotiating a price for his help on our trip to Tofua Island. From our time on Niuafo'ou, we now know what to include in conversations when talking to the locals, especially repeatedly mentioning how beautiful the island is and how delicious the food tastes. We also know what not to include, which is any mention of our equipment and possessions, as this causes jealousy and widens the divide. When people ask about it, we say it all belongs to the University and that we are poor like them.

Our praise of the island and its food does involve a bit of a white lie. To us, it is an example of overexploitation and lack of resources. About 200 people—far too many—live on this island that you can circumnavigate on foot in about an hour. The soil lacks nutrients and only supports the growth of manioc, the root most tolerant of suboptimal growing conditions. Even breadfruit trees don't grow roots here. The locals mainly eat fish, octopus, and mussels, but they often break off the whole coral when harvesting mussels. Many corals seem damaged. The few pigs on the island look skinny, and there are too many mangy dogs running around in packs, barking non-stop.

The wife of Afah sits outside the house to prepare the next meal, surrounded by flies. Her fingers switch between pushing some raw fish into the mouths of one of her seven kids and pushing the rest of the fish, heads and bones included, into banana leaves so she can cook it in the earth oven. Dogs and pigs repeatedly stick their snouts into the cooked food before Afah serves it to us, together with some octopus and raw fish. Having watched this, we are hesitant to eat much of the meal offered, even though we know how well-meaning our host family is.

It turns out we can't get out of eating the offered feast because Langi, the sister of Afah, scrutinises us. She invites us to her house and observes every one of our moves and every bite we eat. We now remember what we have learned about Tongans' social status on Niuafo'ou: The father's sister, i.e., the paternal aunt, is often the highest-ranking member of any extended family and considered a dignified leader. Langi clearly knows her status, and her stern looks make it clear that we, too, have to follow her orders. Poor Ivo has sworn never to eat octopus because he finds the suckers too disgusting, but Langi orders him to eat the octopus arms, including all their suckers. We both vehemently refuse to eat the raw fish, though, knowing how many parasites and fly larvae we would consume.

Langi immediately turns down our plan to stay in our tent, and we have to sleep in her bed, joined by the bedbugs and fleas that soon start bothering us. The children of the family all have big welts on their skin, obviously from these little blood-sucking bedmates. As is the custom in Tonga, all property is shared, and Langi soon borrows my toothbrush, hairbrush and soap without asking and before I have even noticed. My cup tastes a bit fishy when I drink from it, and only then do I realise that Langi has used that too, right after her midday snack of raw fish.

So far, we have accepted the strong influence the missionaries had and still have on Tongan life. I must admit that here on Kotu, though, we think they could do better. There are three large churches on the island: the Mormons, Wesleyans, and the Free Tongan Church. While the missionaries focus on establishing churches and collecting money from the locals, they seem to invest little in educating the people. Some basic understanding of hygiene would considerably improve their health and quality of life, as would help with growing crops and harvesting seafood more sustainably.

Afah declares that we will travel to Tofua Island on Monday, so we spend a Sunday with him and his family. We have no choice but to attend the Mormon church service with them. I dig out the only skirt I own from the bottom of my bag, which still smells of goat droppings from the ferry. Langi inspects the skirt and declares it unsuitable. Somehow, I haven't noticed how thin and worn the fabric has become. She presents me with one of her petticoats and requests that I wear that underneath—no need to think about when she might have washed it last. There is no need to think either during the three-hour-long church service in the Tongan language, as my only focus is not falling asleep. Naively, we assume that this is our only church duty done for the day, but it's not. Someone owns a video camera and has filmed the whole service, including the people attending church. In the afternoon, we all have to watch that film, projected onto a white sheet on the wall. The locals laugh out loud when someone's face appears on the screen, especially ours.

On Monday, Afah first declares that the weather isn't good enough for traversing the sea to Tofua Island. We spend more time sitting around. We don't push him to leave, as we want the trip to be safe, but suddenly he changes his mind because the wind direction has changed. It doesn't take long before we both lie flat in the small cabin of his boat. The waves are high, and we feel rather seasick until half an hour later when the boat suddenly slows down. Judging by the faces of Afah and his mates, it appears that they have lost their way. Fog has set in, and we can't see the silhouette of Tofua Island in the distance anymore. Afah pulls out his 'Tongan compass': a rope that he throws out the back of the boat. The method is simple: from Kotu to Tofua, you always have to sail straight ahead. You watch the rope, and if it is straight, so is your direction. The only slight problem with this method is that we have already lost our straight route. Our second helper, Tavite, gets out his radio and tries to get some reception. He plans to turn the radio and listen to where the strongest reception comes from. This direction is where the South lies, because the radio station is to the South. The problem with this method is that there isn't any reception at all. Not keen on getting lost, Ivo pulls out his compass and map. After returning to our North-West route, we realise that we will likely need to leave one of our two compasses with Afah, along with the snorkel mask, knife, and soap he has already asked us for.

Soon, the fog lifts again, and we can see the highest mountain in Tonga—the 1,100-metre high Kao, a steep volcanic cone, uninhabited and not far from Tofua. Its silhouette is impressive, like a giant green and black triangle placed into the sea. Also intriguing is the thought that right here, at roughly this location, a well-known historic event took place: the mutiny on the Bounty, an English navy vessel. This mutiny, featured in several famous movies and books, occurred in 1789. While on a mission to transport breadfruit from Tahiti to the West Indies, Captain Bligh ruled his sailors under harsh restrictions, with daily punishments as part of the regime. Bligh's mission was to collect breadfruit as a valuable food source for Britain's slaves in the Caribbean colonies. Tired of the restrictions, acting lieutenant Fletcher Christian seized control of the ship and set the captain and 18 loyalists adrift in the ship's open launch. In an astonishing act of battling the elements, Bligh managed to navigate more than 6,500 km in the small launch to reach safety. The mutineers sailed to Tahiti and even Pitcairn, where they settled before being killed by locals, or each other. By the time Bligh returned to bring the mutineers to justice, only one of them remained on Pitcairn.

With our compass in hand, Captain Afah now safely guides us to Tofua, where a surprise awaits: the island isn't uninhabited, as we were told, but home to two families. Afah informs us that officially, the island is considered uninhabited because one of the earlier Tongan kings had relocated all inhabitants to other places. At that time, white men came to the Pacific to engage in a horrible practice called 'blackbirding,' which involved kidnapping islanders and selling them into slavery, mainly in South America. People from the outer islands like Tofua were in particular danger of being kidnapped and were thus forced to relocate. It appears, though, that some families have returned because Tofua's soil is so much more fertile than that on coral islands. They accept the remoteness in return for growing breadfruit, root vegetables, more coconuts, and kava, which they also sell to the main island. As a result, their pigs are fatter, and the kids look healthier. They also don't even have to worry about getting tobacco from elsewhere, as they are Mormons and aren't allowed to smoke.

Afah wants to alert the locals to our imminent arrival but doesn't have a horn on his ship. So instead, he pulls out a large Kauri shell and produces an impressive sound by blowing into it. Soon, a few people gather on a rocky platform that protrudes into the sea, similar to the 'harbour' on Niuafo'ou. Strong hands pull us ashore whenever the right wave moves the boat into the correct position. Our luggage follows, before Tavite drives the boat to anchor it in the only small bay with a sandy beach. Here, he pulls it up to safety and makes his way through the bush before he rejoins us in a large concrete building that was once the local school and is now intended to become our base on the island.

The former teacher of this school is the head of one of the remaining families. He speaks good English, and so does his son Tokoni, who surprises us with his fluent English and understanding of Western culture. Tokoni has travelled to the US three times to sell kava and settle there but found life in the US too complicated and hectic. Now, at the age of 27, he has returned to this remote place to start a family. His wife, mother of two children, does her best to spoil us with a local delicacy: turtle meat with yams. We hardly get time to eat and digest the thought of having to eat an endangered animal because Tokoni and all the others keep asking why we are here. They find it hard to understand why we would travel from the other side of the world to visit this volcano and search for hot spots in the soil. We have to explain our mission several times but still earn blank looks from most of them. Tokoni seems to understand a bit better, and he springs into action to organise our two-week stay in the inner crater near the small active vent. Captain Afah has suddenly left without a goodbye, even though we have paid him to stay with us for two weeks. Apparently, there is a family emergency at home. So we offer to pay other helpers. Tokoni, Tavite, and another strong neighbour, Aberto, agree to accompany us on the next day's expedition into the caldera.

Now that we know of the human settlements on this island, our plan to translocate the Malau to an uninhabited island doesn't apply here. But if there are warm spots for incubating Malau eggs in the inner caldera, these would be far from the small settlement and separated by a 400-metre high crater rim in an uninviting place where, according to Tokoni, the locals hardly ever venture. The human population is small and would thus pose a minor threat to the birds or their eggs, and they have plenty of other food to eat. Given these considerations, we decide to go ahead with our plan to search for warm soil in the inner caldera. Besides, Afah has left with the boat anyway, so we don't have many other options.

The following morning, our team of five, and a pack of dogs, begin the climb up the 400-metre high crater rim. While we struggle with the steep hill, the three men scamper up the incline without pause, exertion or even a sign of perspiration. They insist that I don't carry anything, which gives me more time to take in the fascinating views from the top. It almost seems as if someone has combined a photo of the barren moon with a picture of a lush Amazon jungle and then placed it all next to a beautiful lake. The moon part of the picture also contains a smoking mini volcano—raw, volcanic power. The view is truly breath-taking. So is the smell, literally, when the wind carries the smoke from the mini volcano in our direction. The sulfuric gases from the volcano smell like rotten eggs or the scent of a thousand extinguished matches. Even the dogs, with their sensitive noses, howl and need some encouragement to follow us. It looks like we will have to put up with this stench for the next two weeks, and we can only hope the wind doesn't blow our way.

Slowly, we descend into the caldera, partly through brittle lava stone, partly through the dense bush where a machete is an essential tool to help create a path. After pitching our tent near the crater lake, in the fiery presence of the volcano, we share some corned beef with our helpers, say goodbye, and thank them many times. They haven't once complained about carrying our heavy gear up and down that steep crater rim, and Tavite doesn't even have proper shoes. He walked the whole way in his thongs.

Over the next few days, we have one main goal: finding warm areas in the soil suitable for the incubation of Malau eggs. There surely must be such spots somewhere with a smoking volcano and a crater lake next to us. We dig and dig, measure and measure, but to no avail. The putrid smell of the volcano makes us loathe the times when the wind blows in our direction. Luckily, chicken-like birds like the Malau don't possess a strong sense of smell, so they would be all right if brought here. Also, some of their close relatives live on other active volcanoes, such as the island of Rabaul near New Guinea.

Digging is hard work, and due to the heat, it is only possible in the early morning and late evening. During the day, the sun burns down onto the lava fields with such force that we can only retreat into the shady forest, where we admire the surreal, partly moon-like landscape around us and freshen up in the crater lake. We fight boredom with newly invented games, such as building stone men out of lava stones, a spear-throwing competition, and an investigation into how far we can let boulders roll down the steep inner crater walls. Tavite brings us fresh water and food supplies twice during these two weeks and cheers us up with his happy laughter about our Tongan language skills and his amazed looks at our futuristic-looking tent and other equipment.

21

A Return Trip with Obstacles

After two weeks, we have to concede defeat. There doesn't seem to be any warm soil in Tofua's caldera, at least not in the fifty or so spots where we have dug holes up to one metre deep. As a last resort, we even climb into another small crater that no longer smokes, not far from the smoking one. Its caldera is densely packed with tree ferns, scrub, and rotting wood. During our descent, we need to forge a path with quick hacks of our machete and feel as if we are in a landscape out of the *Jurassic Park* movie, minus the dinosaurs. Our sweaty effort is to no avail as we cannot find any warm soil down there either. It is time to retreat to the small settlement and leave this bizarre landscape and our smelly neighbour behind. On our return climb to the main crater rim, we almost lose our way on several occasions but eventually find the path we took. We can't help but admire the amazing views from the rim again, this time in soft evening light, where the colours of the caldera assume a depth of intensity not found outside the tropics. The views are so distracting that we lose track of time and arrive at our base in the old schoolhouse after dark. Luckily, we don't believe in the *tevolo*!

The next day, we realise that we have made a big mistake. We have paid Afah all his salary for helping us in advance because he begged us to do so and claimed he needed it to fill his boat's tank. Now, Afah is gone and doesn't exactly have much incentive to pick us up again. Our only hope is the solar-powered phone that the teacher has wisely installed on the island. Its reception is sometimes strong enough to call the neighbouring islands, and this is what we ask Tokoni and Tavite to do. Not once, not twice, but several times a day. Finding out the whereabouts of Afah is somehow entertaining, but it also triggers the scary thought of being stuck on Tofua Island for weeks. The entertainment stems from the stories that Afah invents. First, he can't come to the phone because he has hurt his leg, then he needs to go somewhere to help people prepare an earth oven. Soon after, he has run out of fuel and needs to take his sick daughter to the hospital. In between, the guy who manages the phone is first at lunch, then away from the phone for other reasons. There is not enough sun to operate the phone whenever he is present. Days go by, and there seems to be little hope of Afah picking us up as promised.

While waiting for any news obtained over the phone in the schoolhouse, we chat for hours with our helpers. I wouldn't mind talking to Tokoni's wife too, but she doesn't leave her palm-frond hut, doesn't speak any English, and feels too shy to talk to me. Tavite, in contrast, loves chatting with us. He is very amused by our pronunciation of the Tongan language. For example, we confuse the word for resting with the word for toilet. Resting is *maloló*, with the pronunciation of the last *o*, whereas toilet is *málolo*, with an accent on the *a*. Again and again, Tavite keeps reminding us of this mistake with a big grin on his face. He will probably also talk about it in his home village for weeks to come. We also try to join in with all his other jokes, as it is the laughing that bridges the gap between our cultures most. For two days, the central joke is that one of the dogs looks like Tokoni. Another pun comes closer to the truth and is based on the fact that the locals sometimes, at night, hear big thunder-like rumbling sounds from the caldera and then also see a bright shine over the crater rim of the island. They think that this is when the volcano is more active than usual and spits out bits of lava. The joke is that we didn't get roasted while sleeping down there. We are only glad that we didn't know about this awesome might of the volcano before our two-week stint in the caldera.

Conversations with Tokoni are at a different level, as his education and travels have provided him with more insights into the broader world outside this island. He even dares to express his doubts about the benefits of the Tongan monarchy. Monarchs have reigned over this island nation since 1845, and Tokoni does have some doubts about the absence of a democratic voting system[1]. Another conversation with Tokoni touches our hearts. After some days, he confesses that the teacher is not his biological father. Tokoni was one of those Tongan babies whom their parents gave away as a gift to a person of higher

---

[1]. Since then, in 2008, the then-King, his Excellency George Tupou I relinquished most of his powers and chose to be guided by the Prime Minister of Tonga on most matters of national significance.

status. In his case, this esteemed person was the teacher on Tofua. Tokoni's biological father, a man with a big beard, lives on Ha'apai and has fourteen other children. This father thought Tokoni would have a better future if he lived with a teacher who had only three kids. Tokoni tells us how much he hates his father for giving him away, which shows us that this Tongan tradition of gifting kids can come with psychological side effects.

Our tinned food gets swapped for yams as another week goes by, and Tokoni also presents us with a roasted pig. In the absence of a doctor, we apply first aid to both Tavite and Tokoni's son. Tavite has cut his hand with the machete, and the wound is infected. Our antibiotic cream and a clean bandage help. He can't move his thumb and would need to see a doctor, but Tavite says he wouldn't visit one even if one were available. Tokoni's son has infected mosquito bites all over his legs, and here too, the same cream provides relief. We ask Tokoni why they don't sleep under a mosquito net, which would be a necessity for us. His simple reply is that he doesn't have one. Instead, if there are too many mosquitoes, he gets up in the night and makes a fire outside the thatched hut, hoping that the smoke will deter the biting beasts.

There is no mosquito net, but a big portable cassette player with enormous loudspeakers can be found. It is about a metre long, and Tokoni somehow dragged it back from his time in Los Angeles. He hasn't had batteries to run it for years, but luckily, we have some spare ones for our torch that he can use. Tokoni beams with joy because he can finally play his only tape again: the Beatles. This moment will remain in our memories—sitting outside a palm-frond hut on a remote island with a smoking volcano, stuck for an undetermined time, and listening to *Yellow Submarine* and *Yesterday* from an enormous cassette player. Not far from us, the sun sets over a sea that looks rather rough to us, with waves breaking against the rocky shoreline with such force that it sounds like thunder.

We have been waiting for ten days now and keep asking Tokoni to find Afah over the phone. Tokoni is starting to get annoyed with us and also offended. To a Tongan, if the situation is not suitable for undertaking a particular task, you wait for the problem to disappear. You simply live on Tongan Time and don't try to jump through hoops to get it done. Also, Tokoni sees our persistence as a sign that we are not happy with the food and accommodation he provides. We try to explain that we need to visit the next island, Late, and that we are under time pressure to carry out this translocation before our funds run out. But we are not sure whether he agrees.

To top our concerns, while listening to our little radio, we hear a strong storm warning for the whole Vava'u group of islands. Vava'u is to the north, and the storm is moving south, i.e. towards us. But all of a sudden, the kids jump up and shout, "*Vaka, Vaka!*"—"boat, boat!" They have heard the sound of someone blowing the kauri shell at sea. Never have we packed up our equipment so quickly. We hand over our last supplies and mosquito net to Tokoni and his wife, and off we run to the small rock. The rocky platform had served as a landing spot for the boat when we arrived, but not today, unfortunately.

The waves are much higher than when we first arrived, and the boat captain does not come anywhere near the rocky shore. He is not willing to risk his boat being broken on the rocks and may also not be as skilled in landing here. We only now notice that it is not Afah steering the boat but another man from Ha'apai. He has a thick beard, unusual for Tongans, and we watch as Tokoni almost freezes upon seeing him. This man might be his birth father, as Tokoni's facial expression resembles hate for that very moment.

We don't have much time to think about Tokoni's emotions, though, as we have some swimming to do. Tavite has already jumped into the water with his injured hand and paddled to the boat. The captain steers it a bit closer to the rocky platform so that Tokoni can throw our equipment to Tavite. Some pieces land on the deck, but some in the water, and we have no idea how Tavite somehow manages to fish it all out of the foamy waves. I think he uses a long stick, but I don't have time to watch as now it's our turn. Tokoni asks me to take off my shoes and points towards the water. There is not much time to be afraid. I step from the platform into the uninviting waves with all my clothes on. The waves break over me, but somehow, I keep paddling, avoiding being thrown onto the rocks, and I keep looking up to see where the boat is through my fogged glasses. Finally, after what seems like an eternity in a hell of waves, some strong hands pull me up into the boat. Ivo soon follows, and the captain once again moves closer to the platform so that Tokoni can throw over our boots. We only have a few seconds to wave goodbye to him, tears of farewell emotion on both his and our faces, before the boat turns away from the coast.

The trip back to Kotu is fast, as the waves and wind are behind us. We overhear the captain talking to Tavite in Tongan, saying Afah was too afraid to make this trip. Back at Kotu, we once more admire the colours in the coral reef, then we are once more invited by Langi. I politely decline when she offers her clothes for me to get changed into. She grumpily accepts but insists that instead, we wash our feet, face, and hair in front of everyone nearby, much to the amusement of our onlookers. Our clothes have already dried, and all I want is to leave this island and return to Vava'u for a shower and a proper bed. Luckily, a ferry destined for Vava'u is due to arrive at Ha'apai at midnight tonight. First, though, we have to have a word with Afah.

Our former captain twists the story. How great of him to stick to his promise to have us picked up, and that it is our fault that we wanted to leave Tofua Island in such a hurry. We could respond that he didn't stick to the deal when he left the island instead of staying with us and that we got picked up much later than discussed, but we don't argue long with this man who speaks English but has such different views on commitment and timing. Our only response is not to hand over one of our snorkel masks. We do present him with our compass, knife, and other smaller bits and pieces as promised but feel the mask is not warranted. This refusal creates an awkward situation, as Afah becomes a beggar. He keeps coming back to ask us for the mask, and doesn't want to accept "no". I feel angry and stubborn, but Ivo gives in and hands over the mask to him. His leniency is probably the better approach, as it gives Afah an incentive to take us back to Ha'apai, from where we need to catch the ferry to Vava'u.

At Ha'apai, we have a few hours to spend before the scheduled departure at 2 am. Another one of those nightly boat departures. Afah invites us to join him in a friend's palm-frond hut, but for now, we have had enough of the Tongan lifestyle and being stared at, and we just want to get back to our Hilltop Guesthouse. The cabin of the boat becomes our terminal during the wait. We are about to nod off when a group of teenagers, about 16 years old, decide to swim over and violently rock our boat. Ivo has fun playing with them the Tongan way, which mainly involves making fun of others in their presence. He first stares at them, and they stare back. Then he grimaces and yells out in Tongan: "Huh, come here, pālangis like to eat boys!" First, the boys retreat, entirely shocked, but then we can read two emotions on their faces. One is surprise, the other is respect that a pālangi can joke with them in their language. They have the best giggle when Ivo pulls out a fork and points at one of them, luring him to the boat with his winking finger. Soon they leave us alone, and we fall into an exhausted sleep on a makeshift mattress made out of our life vests.

Around midnight, a man wakes us from a deep sleep by stomping around on top of the cabin. He completely ignores us, pokes around in the water with a long stick, and rattles on the anchor chain. Are we being abducted? Our attempts to start a conversation yield no success, and he soon gets off the boat and wades back to shore. Later, we find out that Afah had sent him to take the boat to a deeper spot in the reef as the tide was receding. His friend did not want to explain his actions to us, for unknown reasons.

There is no chance to go back to sleep, our life vests are not the most comfortable mattresses, and the excitement of catching the big ferry named Olovaha soon mounts up. Indeed, two hours later, someone calls out from one of the other many boats that we now see anchored all around us. The ferry lights appear as two tiny bright stars in the far, far distance. All the surrounding boats contain people from nearby islands waiting for the vessel. People chat from boat to boat, and there is lots of laughter and action. We are surprised again by how active Tongans are at night, but this is not too surprising given how much they sleep during the heat of the day. All around us, the sea starts glimmering from bioluminescent bacteria, and the many torch lights from people in the boats add to the fireworks.

Once anchored, the Olovaha first needs to be unloaded. In a somewhat chaotic way, people throw all kinds of items into small boats. This delivery is the only reliable supply of goods for many people from the small surrounding coral islands. Afah has rejoined us to steer our boat closer. We need to wait for an hour or so before we can finally board, then slump into the first available seats. A matron of a large family feels pity for us and kindly offers watermelon and crackers, which we thankfully accept. We must look rather desolate in our dirty, salt-encrusted clothes, uncombed hair, and overall exhaustion. Later, I can't remember much about the 13-hour trip to Vava'u as I am in a drowsy state. In Neiafu, we only manage to get off the vessel with the help of the delicious instant coffee we managed to buy at the bar. Coffee that I wouldn't have let near my palate some months ago.

22

On Late Volcano— Mafana, Mafana!

Back in Neiafu, our enjoyment of Western comforts is dampened by a letter from Mr Hopps. He now sets an ultimatum: either we support his plan for a translocation, or he will influence the government to have our visa revoked. Ivo and I have another long discussion and conclude that we can't agree with his plan. Even if we did agree on Fonualei Island as a new home for the Malau, we can't accept that he doesn't want to check this volcano for its suitability or that he wants to use adult birds for the translocation. Also, the yacht that he intends to use is currently cruising somewhere near Barbados in the Caribbean Sea, far away from Tonga. It will take another few weeks for it to arrive here, and we don't want to wait that long.

This bombshell of a letter does depress us for a while, but we are determined to at least check out the next volcano, Late, hoping that it will prove suitable for the Malau. Thus, even though we are unlikely to carry out the translocation without Mr Hopps' help, we can at least finish what we have come to do. Late — pronounced La-tay— is one of those islands in the Tongan archipelago's western 'chain of beads'. Like Tofua and Niuafo'ou, this volcano has a jagged-looking coastline that is more menacing than inviting, and landing there will be a challenge. Like these other two islands, it has a lake, though this one is much smaller and lies inside a pit crater that resulted from an eruption outside the main crater. The last documented eruption on Late occurred long ago, in 1845, which has provided lots of time for vegetation to conquer the island. Aerial pictures show dense forest in most parts, except for the barren top of the central volcanic cone. The extensive areas of established vegetation and the presence of the crater lake make it a likely island for our translocation, but we first need to get there. Late is uninhabited, so we are told, and we need to find someone who occasionally goes there to harvest coconuts or similar produce.

This someone is a man called Salesi, who is a friend of a friend of the wife of Rolf, our Austrian friend from the Hilltop Guesthouse. Alerted through the grapevine by some locals to our offer of a paid trip to Late Island, Salesi makes a separate trip to Neiafu. He lives on the island of Hunga, one of the outermost coral cays of the Vava'u group, and the one closest to Late[1]. Luckily, we happen to stroll around the harbour when Salesi is in town. Somehow, he recognises and approaches us. "Hi, pālangi," he says, "you want to go to Late?"

"Yes," we reply, with a satisfied glance at his fishing boat, which looks quite sturdy and reliable by Tongan standards. We agree on a price for the trip, partly to be paid after our return. Burnt by our experience on Tofua, we also establish that he and another helper will stay with us during our one-week stay on Late, for the entire time. We have no input into the departure time; it is tomorrow, Salesi decides, as he wants to get back to his home island, Hunga. From there, we will depart for Late the day after. "I have been waiting here for a long time," he says, pointing to the jetty near his boat. Neither he nor anybody else had alerted us that he was waiting; we just happened to walk by. "Why didn't you come and see us at the Hilltop Guesthouse?" He does not respond. Obviously, that guesthouse is a pālangi place, and Tongans don't like going there.

This new plan leaves us with one afternoon to gather all our supplies for the one-week stay. If it weren't for Rolf and his connections, we would never have achieved that. So the following day, we are off to an island again, this time crossing about 15 km of open sea in a fishing boat. The trip gives us time to bridge the cultural gap with Salesi, but we realise there is less bridging required than in previous chats with Tongans. His English is good, and he is pretty open-minded about the world outside his tiny island. He seems to understand why we want to go to Late and seems proud that he can be involved in a project to help save the Malau.

---

1. This is a different island to the volcano named Hunga Tonga—Hunga Ha'apai with violently erupted in January 2022 and caused widespread destruction *https://www.abc.net.au/news/2022-01-22/satellite-data-images-reveal-power-of-tonga-volcano-eruption/100773458*

On Hunga, Salesi and his family go out of their way to show excellent hospitality. Well, excellent according to local standards. We would prefer to stay in our insect-free tent, but this is out of the question and would hurt his pride. He, his wife, and their three kids move into a small palm-frond hut and offer us their brick house next door. Sleeping on our camping mats is not allowed either; it has to be in their bed. Its soft mattress is filled with the cotton-like fluff of the seed pods of the Kapok tree (*Ceiba pentandra*). While this feels comfortable at first, the mattress is riddled with fleas, and we don't have enough insect spray left to fight them. So instead, we endure the obligatory bloodsuckers and hope that it's only for one night, as we plan to depart for Late the next day.

The next day runs by Tongan Time. "Maybe tonight," Salesi says, "when the sea is calmer." Off to church again, this time of the Methodist religion. Again, we ponder the discrepancy between the fancy church building and the basic thatched huts where most locals reside, surrounded by garbage, mangy dogs, pigs, and numerous kids. Salesi's wife doesn't speak much English, but another woman, who has been married to an Italian doctor for five years, approaches us. She tells us how horrible it was to live in Italy. Like many Tongan women, she thought she had landed a dream catch when finding a wealthy pālangi man from overseas to marry. This dream obviously wasn't real. She says that during her time in Italy, she was kidnapped once, robbed thrice, and almost killed once. Now she is back in Hunga, without a husband but with a half-Italian baby son, and finds life much better than in Italy.

In the evening, Salesi decides to leave the following day instead. Another night in the Kapok bed. More worrying, though, is one question that Salesi asks us: "Do you have fins to paddle through the surf when we land?" We do have snorkel masks, and Salesi is happy about that, but he is worried that we won't make the arduous swim from the boat to the stony shore without fins. Late's eastern coast, near the crater lake, is too rocky to land the boat, and we will have to swim through the pounding surf. We always knew that and have even brought an emergency beacon in case something goes wrong, but we haven't thought of fins. Let's hope that our experience on Tofua Island has prepared us well enough to paddle through the surf again, even without flippers.

Salesi seems a bit nervous about this trip as well. We agree that if the surf on the eastern side is too rough, he will land on the western side, where a small rock platform makes landing easier. Unfortunately, this location would mean that we would have to battle through a lot of impenetrable scrubs to get to the lake. Paddling for a few minutes in pounding surf seems a better solution than trekking through untrodden bushland for hours.

The following day, ten men board the fishing boat with us. Apart from our two helpers, eight young friends of Salesi have decided to come along for fun and to work on their kava plantation on Late's western side. These men try to hide their curiosity about the pālangi woman who does things that women in their culture are not supposed to do—such as travelling somewhere without another woman by her side, on a fishing boat and on a rather dangerous mission. A lot of joking and chatting helps them hide their curiosity and aids us in bridging the culture gap. The men also catch two large tuna fish with a fishing line and eat some of their meat raw straight away. Unfortunately, I soon become the victim of seasickness, which forces me to lie flat in the cabin for the six hours of our trip. The oily smell of the engine doesn't help combat my nausea, and I can't follow Ivo's frequent requests to come and sit with the others on top of the cabin. Only shortly before reaching Late do I manage to get up, in time to see the rugged black coastline of this island, surrounded by a lot of white surf.

Once anchored offshore, there is little time to be scared. Our second helper, Vaha, swims ashore with his snorkel mask, towing a long rope. The way he scrambles onto the rocks looks almost effortless as if there were no powerful splashing surf surrounding him, and he then somehow ties the rope to a rock. We watch from the rocking boat as two other volunteers pull themselves along the rope to the shore and join Vaha on the big boulder. Then it's our turn. Donning our snorkel masks, we follow them along the rope, wearing all our clothes except for our shoes. The rock where the men are waiting is 2 metres away from the rope's end. From the water, this distance looks like an eternity to me. I let go of the comforting rope and somehow push myself through the surf until I am pulled up by the men's strong arms. Ivo, who is just behind me, doesn't kick hard enough and lands on some other rocks from which he scrambles ashore. He ends up with quite a few bruises, but luckily nothing too serious. We have reached Late at last! Our skillful helpers tie our waterproof barrels, bags with food, and two 20-litre canisters of water to a buoy and swim all of that luggage ashore as well. The only casualty is the bag with bread, which has been soaked by the waves and will need to be eaten quickly before mould sets in. We will have to get by with crackers and instant noodles for the rest of the week, but that is a small price to pay for having made it here safely.

After arriving ashore, I almost pass out. The seasickness from the boat, the adrenaline kick from kicking through the surf, and the strong sun cause me to become dizzy. There is no shade in sight, and now, in the middle of the day, the black lava attracts the sun with relentless force. Close to collapsing, I manage to wave goodbye to the other eight men who are taking the boat to the western side and have been so brave in helping us. I also realise that Salesi has jumped back in the water to do some spearfishing, and I find it incomprehensible how he could voluntarily enter that foaming sea again. With my last strength, I drag myself away from the black lava stones into the bushland behind the coast, where my energy slowly returns during a long rest in the shade.

The lake is only 700 m from where we have landed, but it takes us quite a while to get there. Ivo leads with the compass while the two men use their machetes to cut a path and probe the ground. The lava flows have left a surface riddled with holes, some of them covered with a fragile layer of hardened lava. You can break through this layer and risk cutting your skin if you step on it. Our walking time is accordingly prolonged, but we still enjoy the feeling of walking on land that has probably not seen humans for a long time. Salesi and Vaha insist on carrying all the luggage, so we have more time to listen to the various bird calls. Some rare birds thrive on this island, and two of these species occur nowhere else in the world (Tongan Whistler *Pachycephala jacquinoti* and Friendly Ground Dove *Gallicolumba stairii*).

At the lake, we pitch our tents, and the two men walk back to fetch some lava stones, large leaves, and fish. First, though, they brace the pounding surf again to catch more fish with their spears. The stones and leaves they carry are necessary for starting the umu—an earth oven—in which Salesi and Vaha cook a dinner that we will remember for a long time. The fresh fish, prepared without a gall bladder, is tender and delicious, the sweet potato and taro equally good, and the atmosphere unique. So here we finally sit, around an earth oven in dense bushland prepared by our two special survival experts, so far from civilisation and with the only sound coming from the wind and birds around us. Salesi is very interested in birds. Together, we identify the frigate birds that show their mating displays over the lake, the frog-like calls of the ground doves, and the melodious songs of Tongan whistlers and swallows. He also tells us that the weather was very kind to us when we landed today. The surf was unusually mild and the wind favourable for our landing.

Early the following day, the search for warm soil around the crater lake begins. We all dig, and dig, and dig, but all we discover is cold soil. After some hours, we find it hard to keep up our enthusiasm in front of our two helpers, who have started losing interest in digging. We have to dig a hole about one metre deep each time before measuring the temperature. Tongans don't like to do things that seem to make no sense—or are a waste of time. Salesi is such an open-minded man, but even he starts to doubt the purpose of our mission. After ten holes are dug, he and Vaha sit down in the shade, and we all have a long break from digging.

Then, finally, the eleventh hole brings life into our helpers. Vaha is doing the digging, and suddenly, he shouts out loud and excitedly: *"mafana, mafana!"*—"warm, warm." He can feel the warm soil with his hands. The two men, who are so calm and reserved at all other times, join in when we cheer with excitement. They dig furiously, and at one-metre depth, our temperature sensors confirm the fantastic find: the temperature is just perfect, 34 degrees Celsius, for the incubation of Malau eggs. We have found this warm soil in front of a large boulder that sits deep in the earth. It may be that the hot steam from the volcano somehow accumulates in front of this rock. Our subsequent excavations nearby confirm that the whole area near the boulder provides sufficiently warm soil temperatures.

This warm soil is our prize for all the effort of getting here. This area could be the key to helping the Malau survive on another island, protecting it from extinction in the long term. It all seems quite straightforward now that we have detected this potential incubation site, realised that the forests here would be suitable for the Malau, and found two amazing helpers for such trips. In addition, Royal Tongan Airline has recently started flying to Niuafo'ou every fortnight again, and we would be able to transport the eggs rather quickly. If only Mr Hopps's threats to revoke our visas didn't hinder us so much.

Our minds go round and round. My mind races faster than Ivo's, who still feels disheartened by Mr Hopps's threats and the fear of doing this on our own. I can't help but think that we shouldn't let this opportunity for the Malau pass, and soon I have infected Ivo with my enthusiasm. We will do it; we will translocate at least some eggs to this island. Whether Mr Hopps approves or not, we are now so close to achieving this goal. We plan to carry out two translocations, each with 30 eggs. This approach reduces the risk of losing eggs if anything goes wrong, and we can only fit that many eggs in our portable incubator. Ideally, we should translocate more eggs, based on what the experts say about the probability of a new population surviving, but that's all we can achieve, especially without Mr Hopps's help. Maybe the Professor can find another person to take over from us, who can then continue the translocation.

First, we spend more days near the lake to measure vegetation densities and food availability for the Malau. It turns out that both of these are similar here to those on Niuafo'ou and thus make Late suitable for the birds. Also, we investigate which species of rats live in this forest. To our relief, we only find the small Polynesian rats that also occur on Niuafo'ou, not the two larger species of rats which could be predators of Malau eggs or chicks. While we wait for the boat, Salesi and Vaha discover four coconut palms in the dense jungle, a rare find in the dense forest of broad-leaved plants. They cheer with such delight. Tongans and coconut palms are one unit, almost inseparable, and our helpers have felt rather lost without them for these past few days. They are thrilled to find a number engraved in the bark of one of the palms: 1957. Salesi thinks this represents the year when locals last visited this remote part of the island to accompany some surveyors from New Zealand who mapped Late. Underneath the number 1957, he uses his machete to add 1992—the year that commemorates our expedition.

We also find trash that looks suspicious to us: pieces of metal plus an old fuel canister, and we make up stories about how, at some time in the past, a plane may have crashed here without anybody noticing, where people slowly starved to death and all that remained was this fuel canister. But, of course, we are unlikely ever to find out! Then, to his immense delight, Salesi finds a coconut. He amuses us with the many purposes this one coconut serves: the water for drinking, the flesh as an addition to the evening fish soup, and the two halves of the shell as lids for the pot and as cups for serving the soup.

Our last job on this island is to prepare a burrow in which we plan to bury the translocated Malau eggs. First, we dig a burrow, one metre wide and deep, at the location where we have found the warm temperatures, and then confirm with our temperature sensors that it is still warm enough for incubating the eggs. Then, before refilling the hole, we prepare the soil manually. This involves using our hands like a sieve to remove any stones or other sharp objects that could damage the eggs. Finally, we mark the burrow with a long stick.

The time has come to leave this island for now, and we feel a bit sad. It has been wonderful to spend these days here with two men who looked after us so well and were so excited about exploring this part of Late themselves. Only at night were they often scared, as the muttonbirds (*Puffinus pacificus*) and barn owls (*Tyto alba*) would call loudly from nearby, and their sound was somewhat eerie and unknown to the men. They, too, seem to be afraid of the *tevolo*.

On the agreed day, Salesi's friends, who have camped on the opposite side of the island, steer the boat back to where we last jumped off it. They sound the ship's horn, and we venture to the coast and jump into the water, almost as if it were a leisure swim in a city pool. Luckily the waves are not too high today, and the surf is less wild than last time. Still, one swim to the boat is enough for us, whereas Salesi and Vaha keep swimming up and down the coast with their spears to catch more fish. Later they mention that fishing is much easier here, as the fish are less shy due to the lack of experience with humans. Also, the reef around their coral island home is depleted due to overfishing, and they find it hard nowadays to catch any larger fish there.

Instead of heading straight back to Hunga, we stay another night on Late Island, this time on the western side, where the men grow some kava and occasionally visit to harvest this crop. To land here, Salesi has to manoeuvre the boat close enough to the rock platform for us to jump ashore as quickly as we can, glad to land on solid ground and not in the sea. Luckily we have had some lessons in such landing on both Niuafo'ou and Tofua Island.

One thatched hut represents the only temporary accommodation on Late, and Salesi's eight friends busily sweep and clean up their mess from many past stays. Women don't usually visit this place, which could do with some cleaning indeed. The men are aware of that and want to do justice to my unusual presence. Their mess consists of piles of coconut shells and the shells of a large land crab called the coconut crab, locally known as 'U'u (*Birgus latro*). It is the largest terrestrial crab on Earth, the largest existing land arthropod altogether, measuring about 1 metre from leg tip to leg tip and weighing about

4.5 kg. These enormous crabs can climb coconut palms and crack the hard nuts with huge pincers. They have been hunted to extinction on other islands but are still abundant here and a welcome snack for the occasional visitors. The men only have to be careful not to get pinched when catching them. Apparently, this hurts like hell.

We hand over our last few tins of corned beef, which the men devour with immense joy. One man, in particular, eats with an infectious smile. He carries the unusual name 'Manu Foster.' Manu means an animal, and Foster is a beer brand from New Zealand that is occasionally available in Tonga, so this chap is the 'Beer Animal'. Maybe his parents thought of this creative appellation over a bottle of beer while they tried to drown their frustration about a baby that cried like an animal? Ivo and I are having fun imagining several other possible explanations for this choice of name and marvel once again at the fascinating appellations found in Tonga.

Our food exchange is a good deal for all, as the men prefer corned beef, while we favour the fish and coconut crab they provide. After dark, poor Ivo can't escape another kava session, as this is what the men always do when visiting Late. After all, the kava can't get any fresher than here, and apparently, it is one of the most delicious ones in Tonga. 'Delicious' is relative for Ivo, who struggles to swallow the hallucinogenic, earthy, and bitter-tasting drink. Today, the men make an exception for me that they have probably never made before: I am allowed to watch the kava ceremony from my seat while leaning against the wall of the hut. They can't really send me out in the dark; there is no other hut to go to, and they don't allow me to sit in our tent by myself—the *tevolo* might catch me! Women, except virgins, are usually excluded from the kava ceremony, and I thus feel honoured to watch. The show is very entertaining indeed: ten Tongan men singing traditional songs and giving a performance that would beat some opera at home. Soprano, Alto, and Tenor voices combine in beautiful harmony while voicing time-honoured songs passed on through generations. The emotional songs are mainly about the wind, fishing, and love, of course. Two men wear beanies because the temperature has dropped to 20 degrees Celsius at night, much too cold for Tongans. Two of their mates smoke tobacco out of the hollow legs of a dead crab. The whole hut smells of burnt chitin, the chemical contained in this unusual cigarette holder.

The following day, we pack up our tent in a hurry as the men are ready to go. Their luggage consists of a small bundle of clothes, machetes, large bags full of lava stones for the earth oven at home, and even larger bags full of kava, coconuts, and roots. The fishing boat seems alarmingly overloaded, but we are the only ones worried about the proximity to the sharks beneath. The wind is behind us and carries us back to Hunga in only five hours. I join the men on the cabin roof, less seasick than last time, and we admire some humpback whales passing close by. Shortly before Hunga, Salesi signals the okay to finish up the last supply of water crackers that we had kept as a reserve should the boat ever go adrift or the engine stop. We are amazed by his foresight in keeping this food for so long, as it contradicts what we experienced in Tonga before. Food is usually eaten straight away. Salesi also talks a lot to us about the translocation and comes forward with some good ideas for making it as smooth as possible. He is definitely the right man to help us achieve our goal, and we are so grateful to have met him.

At Hunga, we say goodbye to our cheerful crew, and they hand us a bag full of pomelos, the largest of all citrus fruits, as a present. Salesi gets out his emergency sail and uses it to create a shade cover on top of the cabin for us. The three of us continue to Neiafu, and before we disembark, this generous and courteous man hands us his goodbye present: a 1-metre-long tuna fish that he had caught in the surf around Late Island and kept fresh on ice in his cooler box on board. We know how valuable this present is for him because he gets paid very little for his fish from the fishing cooperative, and it is hard for him to make a living from it. However, we also know we can't refuse the present without hurting his pride, so we accept gratefully and reiterate how much we are looking forward to carrying out the first translocation with him.

23

Meeting the Minister— In Tongan Time

At our Hilltop Guesthouse in Neiafu, Rolf and his wife Lautoka happily prepare the fish for us all. Over dinner, our first sitting at a real table in weeks, they update us on all the news from Neiafu. The main update on local gossip is that Alex has finally met a Tongan girl he can date. Alex is a Swiss guy who works for Rolf. For months, he has tried to meet a Tongan girl. His attempts were hindered by Tongan custom, which allows unmarried women only to meet men in the presence of either their mother or another older woman. These sentinels watch over every word being said. Such an arrangement was not to Alex's liking, nor was the only other way of finding a girl, which would be to dishonour her in the bushes and then be forced to marry her afterwards. Andy also wants to stay in Tonga, which does not speak in his favour. If you are a pālangi and wish to return to your home country, you are more likely to find a Tongan girl to join you, as many women want to leave for this promising world outside their island home. We don't know how exactly Alex navigated the dating circus, but somehow, he did, and we are happy for him.

While the gossip is entertaining, we have a more critical problem to solve. Mr Hopps's threat to revoke our visa weighs heavily on our minds, and we want to be pre-emptive and obtain a permit from the Minister of Lands to translocate Malau birds to Late Island officially. This permit is Rolf's idea, who has lived here for so long, knowing how Tongan politics are played and how important family bonds are in this country. The Minister's official name is 'Minister of Lands, Survey and Natural Resources', and the unprecedented translocation of Malau could thus fall under his jurisdiction. His daughter resides in Neiafu, and Rolf recommends visiting her to present our case. Rolf doesn't believe that the conservation of Malau should be the only drawing card. Instead, we should also emphasise what a tourist attraction the Malau on Late could be and how this would bring tourist dollars to Vava'u. Rolf's plan works out. We visit the daughter, chat for a while about the benefits of our mission and hand over a present. She then organises an appointment with her father on the main island for us.

Our plan means travelling to Nuku'alofa, but this time we will take a plane instead of a rusty swimming coffin of some sort. At least we can use our time in the capital to buy new clothes and books. After an uneventful flight and settling into a hotel, we race to town to get these things done, then head to the minister's office, only to discover that he works by Tongan Time. At the time mentioned by his daughter, there is no minister to be seen. "He is not coming in today," a secretary informs us, "please return the next day at 11 am." This story repeats itself the day after. We come back the day after once more, and indeed, this time, we only have to wait for an hour before the minister arrives in his black Mercedes Benz.

He looks rather old, and when we are allowed to enter the room, we first have trouble spotting him. The honourable minister sits sunken in an impressive leather chair behind an enormous mahogany desk containing a giant pile of files and loose paper. We address him with 'Mister Honourable' and sit down on the allocated chairs as we are told, 3 metres from the desk. His secretary gestures for me to speak, and I stand up and present our case. Meanwhile, the Honourable Minister flicks through a file, remaining silent. No word from him in what seems like an endless pause. Then he finally starts speaking, but his voice is so soft that we can't understand a word. Eventually, the secretary leads me closer to the mahogany desk, where I can barely make out the Minister's decree. "We are grateful for what you are doing for Vava'u," he says, with a stern look on his face, "I will give you exclusive rights to use Late Island for translocating the Malau." He then hands us a handwritten letter on official-looking paper in which he confirms this decision. The letter, in English, has a few spelling mistakes but will nevertheless be worth gold should we ever have to fight for our visa.

24

Ana e Ivo Malau

In late April 1992, we return to Niuafo'ou but find that we must spend our first weeks back smoothing relationships. The roughness has obviously been introduced by an employee of Mr Hopps, who visited during our absence to catch birds for Mr Hopps's zoo. This guy has apparently told the locals all kinds of things about us—as Kailao, the policeman, mentions. The two worst allegations are that we torture the Malau with electric shocks and that we are very unhappy with Malohi as our host. It takes us a while to discover why Malohi refuses to allow his sons to help us carry all our equipment to Motu Molemole. He claims they are all asleep, but Kailao tells us the real reason. The accusations have seriously hurt Malohi's pride. All we can do is quickly reiterate to Malohi how happy we are with him as our host and how much we enjoy living with him. Still, before he believes us, we must climb up and down the steep path to the crater lake several times by ourselves, carrying our tent, boat, 20 litres of water, and barrels full of equipment back to Motu Molemole.

We have included a new battery for Malohi's tractor in the load for the 'swimming coffin' and agreed that in return, Malohi would give us a lift with our equipment during these next few weeks. Unfortunately, he seems to have already forgotten about this deal and may also have used up most of the fuel, which arrived a week ago. So when we first ask for transport, Malohi asks us to pay for fuel. We walk off, showing him how offended we are, and he rushes after us with his tractor to give us the lift. He may have a high social status, but even with Malohi, we sometimes need to put our foot down.

With lots of talking, we also manage to convince Kailao that we are not electrocuting the Malau. Finally, our relationships with him and Malohi become smoother again, and Malohi even bestows upon us the honour of naming one of his new grandkids. The baby boy is already a few months old but still doesn't have a name. We feel honoured but also concerned. Tokoni, on Tofua Island, has made us more aware of the Tongan culture of 'child giving', i.e., bestowing your children to relatives or friends of higher social or economic position. We hope this is not what Malohi intends! Little 'Niki', as we name him after my brother, is repeatedly brought over to me so that I can hold and look at him. I am somewhat concerned that they expect me to adopt him and take him back to Austria, where he would be better off economically.

When locals talk to us or about us, they now call us 'Ana e Ivo Malau'. This new surname somehow indicates they have accepted our close relationship with the birds, and we use it to reiterate the need for conservation whenever we talk to them. Malohi tells us he plans to release pigs on the largest islet in the crater lake, Motu Lahi. This free-range farming would allow the pigs to get fat without running away, and he could come back later to catch them. Unfortunately, his plan would be an ecological disaster for the Malau and other birds, such as shearwaters, nesting and living on that islet. Pigs dig up everything, cause erosion and destroy the vegetation. We manage to convince Malohi otherwise, hoping that he somehow understands our reasoning.

With Malohi's and Kailao's help, we also organise another small conservation success: removing the last two goats on Motu Molemole, as these, too, cause a lot of damage to ecosystems. Following Kailao's push, the local elders meet and decide to catch them. While this decision means that we are disturbed by a group of young hunters, it is good to know that the vegetation will be protected from being eaten for months to come. Again, we can only hope that this islet will not be used as a free-range goat pen again.

Our preparation for the translocation mainly involves digging up burrows and collecting eggs that have already been incubated for a few weeks. Our candling device indicates their age, and we know that the older eggs, in which the embryos are already quite developed, are more tolerant of temperature changes. While we hope to keep the temperature in our incubators at a constant level during the translocation, there could always be unforeseen hiccups with technology and travel times. We therefore only take older eggs to Late Island.

We have an important event to celebrate in-between egg collections: Ivo's birthday. Somewhere in the corner of our hut, I have hidden a bar of chocolate and a bottle of wine for him, and I supplement these presents with homemade cake. I am rather proud of this baking, as I have created my own earth oven Tongan style—a burrow in the sand with two lava stones at the bottom. First, I light a big fire on these stones and wait until it burns to embers, then add more rocks on top. The dough is made of flour, water, a few oats roasted in soy oil, sugar, and the few raisins that I managed to buy in the local shop. I wrap it in banana leaves, place it on top of these stones, and cover it in more rocks and a layer of sand. After one hour, everything is unearthed, and the cake is ready and tastes surprisingly good. Ivo says it is the best birthday meal he has ever had. What better praise could a researcher turned housewife get?

My pride soon takes a knock when we are invited to a Sunday celebration in Mu'a, one of the last and more remote villages along the island road. The festivities begin at church, where the local minister holds a two-hour-long service to collect money for the church's priest, who lives a comfortable life in Nuku'alofa. This time, the collection is aided by three women dressed up as something resembling clowns—colourful dresses with balloons attached. They single out individual people and humiliate them as much as possible, which leads to lots of laughter and the victims donating as much money as they can afford. They don't spare me, but unfortunately, I have no money with me. All I have is a bag of tobacco that I brought to give as a gift to our hosts. The clown ladies throw the collection basket at me while laughing out loud, rolling in the dust in front of me, and the whole church community bursts into laughter. The clowns don't let go until I, in despair, throw the tobacco into the basket. This event will definitely be story material for the locals for years to come.

While the church ceremony doesn't exactly match our idea of a celebration, the subsequent feast does. Finally, we participate in a festivity not guided by strict rules, endless speeches, and formalities. This time, some jolly women carry old car tyres around their waist and drum with their fingers on corrugated iron, producing a beat that encourages others to dance. They smear leftover cake into each other's faces, whirl around our backpacks like a lasso, and use our water canister as a pretend toy gun. The laughter and dancing become more and more boisterous, and one of the women even dares to give Ivo a quick kiss. For a moment, I can't help but feel a bit scared, as in this remote village, we are far from the protection that Malohi and Kailao usually grant us, and the ladies take the local tradition of making fun of someone in their presence quite far. Nevertheless, we do our best to join in and laugh at all the jokes, glad that they don't also pull apart our backpacks as part of their joyous dance.

Back in Esia, we improve our trading skills. With money being of little use on this island, such expertise can be a survival skill. We practise it with Laaka, the second oldest daughter of Malohi, who owns a palm-frond hut not far from ours. She is 28, doesn't speak any English, has five children, and has lost quite a few teeth. Her cooking methods are more hygienic than Emeni's, especially because she prevents the pigs from entering the cooking house. Someone tells her that we have a fishing hook in our luggage. Our mastery of the Tongan language has recently improved, and we use this to ask her for a meal. In return, she immediately asks whether she could have the hook, plus a bit of the yeast we still have for baking our pancakes. Knowing that these two things are worth more than one breadfruit meal, we also request a small loaf of bread and casually ask her whether people here happen to grow any pineapples. When Laaka arrives to hand over the bread and pineapple the next day, she asks for a glass of peanut butter, which we promise in return for some more fruit. Soon we will run out of things to swap, though, and will make do with the food that Malohi's wife Emeni cooks for us every weekend.

On Motu Molemole, we get ready for the translocation by digging up eggs and carefully placing those containing a well-developed embryo into the prepared burrow. Here, in the warm soil, the embryo Malau will keep developing until we are ready to take them to Late Island. All seems to go to schedule until an accident causes us to question our plans. Ivo cuts his leg with the machete while clearing a path on our islet, and our alarm bells go off. In the tropics, wounds can get infected and turn very nasty quickly. Luckily, we didn't give the Professor any of our iodine when he wanted to take it to the Philippines because now it's needed. So, several times a day, we wash the wound with this disinfectant, and we make a sling from the bark of a tree, in which Ivo elevates his limb while lying down. During the first few days, the wound looks nasty, and we are not sure it will heal in time for the translocation. Then, slowly day by day, it starts to seal up, and Ivo is glad to switch from a horizontal to a vertical position more often again.

25

First Translocation to Late Volcano

In September 1992, after a non-stop stay of five months on Tin Can Island, studying the birds and preparing for the translocation, we are finally ready to take the eggs to Late. This time, with our precious egg cargo, we hope not to travel in Tongan Time. On the day of our departure, luck is with us, as for a change, the early morning flight is not cancelled or delayed. After we remove the 32 eggs from their warm burrow on Motu Molemole, they travel with us in warm soil in an insulated bucket, and we arrive in Vava'u on time. Upon arrival, we transfer them to our incubator powered by a car battery. Only the employees of Royal Tongan Airline cause a hiccup when they don't know the arrival time of their own planes. Salesi had asked them beforehand, and they told him a much later arrival time. This misinformation means that Salesi is still on his Hunga island while we wait in Neiafu. Luckily, our good friend Rolf is willing to help. He races us from the airport to the harbour and finds another fisherman who is about to depart for Hunga. A slight delay arises when that fisherman needs to wait for his uncle, and the uncle then needs to return to town to find his hat, but overall, we arrive in Hunga only about an hour later than planned.

Salesi and Vaha are as reliable as we hoped and ready to leave straight away for Late, together with the same friends as last time. The sea is not particularly rough but shaky enough to make us seasick. We are quite a sight: both lying flat, each with one Malau chick in a little cotton bag, tucked warm under our jackets. The two little guys couldn't wait and hatched on the trip, not knowing that they would be the first Malau ever to touch the soil of Late. First, though, eggs and chicks have to be brought ashore unharmed, and only Salesi's master skills in boating and landing enable us to do so. The wind has turned in the wrong direction, and we can't land where we did last time. Salesi navigates to a place 10 minutes further up the shore, choosing a large boulder as a landing rock. He throws the anchor, and the other volunteers simultaneously pull on the anchor and rev the engine to get close enough so that Vaha and Salesi can jump onto the rock. We wait at the bow and pass over the container with eggs and chicks when the right wave lifts the boat. It is pretty risky for both the eggs and the boat, but our precious cargo gets to shore safely. Then, we too jump onto the rock, not knowing how we did it without falling, and the volunteers throw our luggage ashore without dropping it into the surf.

The kava farmers take the boat to the western shore while we follow our machete-swinging guides to the lake. The sun burns like hell, and we become exhausted from lifting our legs to scramble over fallen logs and treacherous lava holes, meanwhile keeping the eggs as stable as possible. The chicks travel with us tucked into our shirts again, where they rest as they would usually do in the soil. At the lake, we use our last strength to remove the soil from the burrow we had prepared, carefully place the eggs into their new nest, and cover them with warm soil again. On Niuafo'ou, we have marked the eggs with pencils at the end facing up, and here, we place them in the same position to make sure the chicks hatch right side up and not upside down. Salesi and Vaha help us pitch our tent, and we almost fall asleep over the delicious earth oven dinner of fish and root vegetables they have once more prepared.

Our helpers also find some termites to feed the chicks, and overnight we keep them warm in a small box, provided with food and water, to give them time to fully dry their plumage and recover from the arduous trip. The following day, Salesi has the honour of releasing them. They are alert and ready to conquer their new home. Salesi places them down with sincerity and gentleness. With a proud look on his face, he utters, "A new bird to touch Late's soil!" Off they run, into the next thicket, hopefully as the founders of a new population of Malau.

All we have left to do is prepare a new egg burrow for the subsequent translocation and swim back to the boat. By now, this is almost a routine, even though the surf still looks slightly frightening to us. Sitting on top of the cabin on Salesi's boat is not routine yet, especially when the sea is as rough as today. On the trip back to Hunga, our arms hurt from clinging to the mast, and we struggle to eat our corned beef and cracker while trying not to fall off. Our fellow travellers seem less bothered by the rolling waves, and their singing and chatting cheer us up. What an exhausting and adventurous trip this is, but let's hope it is all worth it!

On Hunga, we have to spend the night on Salesi's island as it is too late to return to Neiafu. Some unexpected entertainment sweetens this in the form of island cinema. Salesi doesn't spend his money on tobacco, like most Tongan men, but on movies, and he has accumulated quite a few VHS tapes in his house. They are mostly action movies with Arnold Schwarzenegger, which I would not watch at home. But here, after not having seen a film for ages, this is such welcome food for our minds. Never mind that the VHS player is operated by a rattling diesel generator that almost drowns the movie sounds and that the children all around us cheer more than loudly every time they observe some action. We both fall asleep halfway through the movie, with all the noise around us, completely exhausted from our first successful translocation trip.

26

You Can Achieve Anything If You Maintain Your Pride!

Back at the Hilltop Guesthouse, our mind-stimulating journey continues when Alex hands over a pile of old German *Spiegel* magazines and three novels that some guests have left behind. We do nothing but read, eat, and sleep for three days. It would be nice to indulge like this for longer, but an unpleasant phone call brings us back to our feet. The secretary of the Prime Minister's Office kindly informs us that Mr Hopps has withdrawn all support for our project and that without his consent, we no longer have any permit to stay in Tonga. She kindly allows us to fetch our belongings from Niuafo'ou before we have to leave the country immediately. The longer we talk to her to find out more details, the more unbelievable the whole story sounds. She provides conflicting information, and we now also remember her name. She is the lady Mr Hopps always uses to sort out all his bureaucratic issues.

After digesting the shock, we call the Professor to ask for help and come up with a plan B. We will change our plan, but not completely, only slightly. Ivo, by himself, will return to Niuafo'ou to fetch the second batch of eggs for the translocation, while I will travel to the mainland to meet at the Prime Minister's Office and consult with Mr Consul. The latter is the German consul in Tonga, whom the Professor knows from his previous trip to Tonga and has now asked for help. We are grateful that the Professor is now entirely on our side and tries to support us despite all the disagreements we have had so far. Hopefully, this consular support, and our permit from the Minister of Lands, will buy us some time to carry out the second translocation and leave the country when we choose to go.

According to the secretary, the Prime Minister's Office will meet in two days to decide on our eviction. I am shocked to hear that the planes to Nuku'alofa are fully booked today and tomorrow. If it weren't for Rolf, who somehow uses his connections to get me a ticket, I wouldn't be able to get to the meeting in time. Leaving for the airport feels strange and unsettling. Ivo and I have taken every step together for so many months, and I don't like it that he will fly back to Niuafo'ou by himself. Let's hope all goes smoothly, and he will be able to return to Neiafu at the same time I plan to return. Ideally, he will come back with eggs and I with a valid visa. We thought about continuing the translocation after we have sorted out the visa issues together, but the cyclone season is approaching, and we thus can't risk travelling any later.

On the flight to the main island, I admire the views from the window. So many beautiful coral islands in a turquoise sea, fringed by white sand, looking like the South Pacific we know from the movies. Landing in Nuku'alofa feels like a big city at first—a tarmac runway, cultivated fields, and coconut palms darkened by the smog of cars. Soon, though, it feels less like Western civilisation when the taxi driver pretends not to have any spare change to earn a higher fare, the traffic is stopped by free-roaming pigs, and the road is fringed by broken-down cars.

In Nuku'alofa, there is barely time to buy some decent clothes before the scheduled meeting at the Prime Minister's Office. Flustered, I arrive there, only to find out that the meeting is not today. Not today at all, not tomorrow, and not the day after either. The secretary who called us in Neiafu gets a bit nervous when I talk to her, and it turns out there never was a meeting scheduled. Now it is more than evident that this woman has given us the wrong information.

Slightly at a loss, I call up Langi, a lady friend of Rolf who is very knowledgeable about the Tongan government. Rolf had already told her about our problems, and she immediately offered to help. While I talk to this educated woman, who is approachable and speaks good English, I notice how much I have missed chatting with other women these last thirteen months. On Niuafo'ou, my primary female contact is Laveni, with her limited English, who is often more interested in the bachelors next door. When meeting the various married women at festivities and church, both on Niuafo'ou and on other islands, I always feel criticised because I don't fit into the typical picture of how a woman is supposed to behave in Tongan society. Langi, in contrast, is more open-minded, has had more contact with Westerners, and is appalled by how Mr Hopps treats us. She has a calm, self-confident aura and reassures me that I shouldn't worry. "You can achieve anything in this world if you maintain your pride," she says. I shall follow her advice!

Through her contacts, Langi finds out what is really happening with our visa. Yes, Mr Hopps has filed a complaint against us, but so far, that is all. No visa withdrawal yet. Langi organises an appointment with a man who sits one step above the secretary in the political hierarchy, and she accompanies me to the meeting. This minister has a file with our case lying on his desk, flicks through it, and demands that we have a meeting with Mr Hopps and the German consul to discuss our issues. How embarrassing: two German scientists squabbling over details for a translocation in front of Tongan politicians. We Westerners are supposed to bring expertise to help countries like Tonga achieve conservation success. Instead, we force Tongan authorities to decide which expertise is better.

During the next two days, I wait for a call from the Prime Minister's Office about the timing of our meeting. In-between, I indulge in the *Friendly Island Bookshop* in town. No call. On the second day, I make my way to the office at 9 am to discover what's happening. It turns out that the secretary 'forgot' to inform me that the meeting would be at 11 am today. It would have been handy for some if I hadn't made it. This news leaves just enough time to inform Mr Consul and pick up a fax letter from the post office that our Professor has sent. It is a well-written plea in which he confirms our expertise, good working attitude, and availability of sufficient funds to support our project.

Slightly nervous at first, I remember Langi's words about pride and enter the meeting room rather calmly and composed. Mr Hopps is already present and doesn't even greet me, while the benevolent Mr Consul welcomes me with a warm smile. The minister tries to make sense of our discussion about which translocation plan is better, but I can see from his face that he can't quite follow us. He is clearly very impressed when I pull out the Professor's fax and the letter from the Minister of Lands. Nevertheless, it is hard to get a sense of where I stand, and I become concerned when I am asked to leave the room. Meanwhile, I can hear Mr Hopps talking loudly inside. Soon, Mr Consul joins me outside and bears good news: we can stay in the country for another six months.

In our letter exchange with the Professor, we have settled on a departure date four months away. He has finally accepted that we won't stay for the entire two years and that we will cut our stay 'short' after 17 months. It was such a fight to convince him that 17 months would be long enough. We are about to carry out our second translocation, Mr Hopps is making it so hard, our equipment is deteriorating, and our physical and mental states are close to exhaustion. The Professor still thinks he will find someone who will continue the project after us—good luck to him. I skip to a travel agent with joy to buy a return ticket to Germany in four months.

Before returning to Neiafu by plane, I stroll along the harbour and discover Mr Hopps's new yacht. In the meeting, he declared that it had finally arrived but admitted it needed repairs. Once these are done, he plans to sail to Niuafo'ou, collect some adult Malau, and take these to Fonualei. He is not willing to change his plan and investigate Fonualei for its suitability first. That fancy yacht looks more comfortable to travel on than the rusty and smelly fishing boats we squeeze into, and I can see why Mr Hopps doesn't want to risk landing it on the rough shores of Late or Tofua.

The flight to Neiafu is made pleasant again by the beautiful vistas of tropical islands in the blue sea. For many people, this view resembles the stuff that idyllic dreams are made of, and the islands look very inviting from above indeed. I ponder how my opinion about paradise has changed after visiting some of them. I have seen the poverty, the amount of garbage lying around, the lack of fertile soil, the destruction of coral reefs by over-harvesting, fleas and bed bugs, and the lack of hygiene. Not the paradise I would like to live in for long unless someone gave me one of those uninhabited islands to rule by myself.

It is nothing short of a miracle when, in October 1992, Ivo and I arrive in Neiafu at about the same time. He has many stories to tell from his time as a single man on Niuafo'ou, but unfortunately, I don't have much energy to listen. The tummy problems that have been bothering me over the last few weeks have worsened, and I have to question my participation in this next translocation. The 31 Malau eggs that Ivo carries with him are indifferent to gastrointestinal problems, and they need to be brought to Late as quickly as possible. We have to make the difficult decision that Ivo must join Salesi and Vaha on his own, as I am just too weak for this arduous trip. Ivo's stories will have to wait, and he leaves on Salesi's boat before I even get to hug him goodbye.

While I try to recover in the Hilltop Guesthouse, well looked after by Rolf and Lautoka, Ivo is in the good hands of Salesi and Vaha. What would we do without all these wonderful people supporting us? Unfortunately, Ivo isn't feeling very fit either today, and it is Salesi who takes charge of the little details that will hopefully make the translocation a success. He ensures the eggs are kept warm in the incubator, gently transferring them to a bucket with warm soil before handing them to Vaha on a rock at the shore, and then they are carefully carried to the lake. He reminds Ivo to measure the temperature again in the burrow we prepared—still perfect for incubation—before bedding this new batch in its new home. In total, 63 eggs (including the two chicks) have now been translocated to Late, hoping that most chicks within them will survive on their new home island. The men are excited to check the eggs we transferred last time—at least six of them have hatched, as evidenced by the numbered eggshell fragments, and another three chicks are digging their way up to the surface. The men keep them warm, provide them with water and termites to eat, and release them when they are dry and agile. We all hope that the other eggs will hatch soon.

After a night in the bush, the three men must find their way through the dense vegetation to the western side of Late. The wind has turned and gathered up some strength, so Salesi's helpers cannot bring the boat to the eastern side, near the lake. This change means rather arduous trekking in brutal heat, and Ivo is beyond exhausted when he swims back to the boat. Nine hours later, after clinging to the mast with his last strength, he lands in Neiafu with clothes stiff from dirt and sweat. In his hand is a goodbye present from Salesi: an enormous tuna fish for dinner.

Back in our hilltop castle, Ivo sleeps for almost 24 hours straight. While my condition has slightly improved, aided by antibiotics that an Italian doctor in Neiafu prescribed, Ivo's stamina remains low. We decide that we need a holiday and book a three-day tourist trip on a yacht, with lots of snorkelling and visits to uninhabited coral islands. Before we start being tourists, Ivo tells me the stories from his solo trip to Niuafo'ou. He was surprised by how the women of Malohi's family were constantly around him. It appears that men in Tonga never cook or care for themselves, and the women made sure he was well fed, dressed and looked after. The ladies could not help but remind him again and again how 'little fat' he is, laughing about this joke for hours. He was also spoilt with the custom pig feast before his departure, followed by the custom shopping lists that Malohi and Kailao handed over to him. This time, Malohi 'only' wants another drum of fuel for his tractor, and Kailao requests a new petroleum lamp. There is a vessel due to leave for Niuafo'ou the next day, just before our tourist yacht departs, and it seems we must spend our dwindling funds on some more presents and supplies for ourselves. Rummaging through shops in Neiafu is not what we feel like doing right now, but we have no choice. The petroleum lamp is relatively easy to find, but the fuel is not, and we ask three suppliers before finally securing a drum of it. Eventually, after a few hours of waiting at the harbour, the supplies are loaded onto another 'swimming coffin,' and we are ready for a holiday.

To us, it feels somewhat surreal to be on holiday in Tonga, and to join the crowds of tourists who visit these tropical cays for snorkelling, lying on a beach, eating fresh seafood and fruit, sleeping on a luxury yacht and experiencing the authentic culture. It feels as if we are stepping onto the other side while, in our minds, we cannot leave the original side behind. Like the Tongans we met, we now regard sunbathing as one of those strange things that pālangis do. The tourists we talk to hold such different views of what life on these islands is like; they compare it to paradise. We don't want to spoil their paradise thoughts with some of our less paradisaic experiences. So we keep our mouths shut, feel out of our element, and try to enjoy the fantastic snorkelling in the coral reefs, the beachcombing on the white collars of uninhabited islands, and the dance display by women on another island. It is the first time we watch traditional Tongan dancing without it being used for money collection at a church. The yacht owner provides fresh seafood that he cooks authentically—in a coconut sauce in the earth oven. Little does he know that we would much rather it be cooked without the sauce. I have already vowed that I will never eat coconut again once I touch German soil.

27

A Cyclone at Last

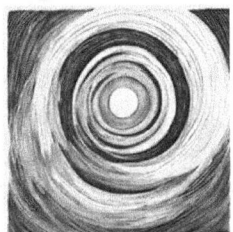

It's November 1992, and upon our flight back to Niuafo'ou and our return to the village, Laveni joins us to convey two important pieces of news. She delivers the first with a big smile on her face: Schweinchen has been slaughtered and will be our welcome feast today, as a thank you for all the presents we shipped and brought along. We try not to show how sad we are. Sorry, Schweinchen, we fed you too well! Second, she and Malohi are pleased that we have become a bit more big and fat in Vava'u. We don't think so, but obviously, this is just a nice thing you say to people when you first greet them.

Unfortunately, our hut has become a partly flooded mess in our absence. The wood borers that have always entertained us with their gnawing sound have finally succeeded, and the thin wooden beams that hold up the woven mats on the roof have partly collapsed. Ivo noticed this happening before he left for the translocation, and he had asked Malohi and his sons to fix it up. Unfortunately, this repair has not happened. We now need to apply our insights into communicating with Tongans to get the job done.

The most crucial insight is never to hurt a Tongan's pride. Blaming them for not doing the job would hurt them and achieve nothing, or worse, the opposite. The second insight is that you use tools such as food, laughter, and joking if you want to get the job done. When Laveni and Malohi's wife, Emeni, come over, we offer a packet of chips and start making jokes about how much Ivo missed me when he was here by himself and how he missed eating the Ofato in Vava'u. Then, casually, Laveni asks me whether Ivo is angry about the flooding in our hut. "Yes," I say, "very angry." And once more, I notice that in Tonga, men have to deal with all such problems, whereas women just joke around, weave mats, cook, and do what men tell them to do. Emeni starts removing weeds from around our house and casually mentions that Malohi will make sure someone will fix the roof soon.

Insight number three also comes to our rescue. You use social pressure to get the job done. We inform everyone we meet during the next few days that our roof has ten holes, even though that's a slight exaggeration, and how we have to start swimming inside our abode now. We are proud that we can convey all of this in Tongan, and the locals find it very funny. This joking builds up social pressure on Malohi's sons, and somehow, within a few days, they climb our roof and fix it in less than an hour.

Our second Christmas with the villagers arrives and with it another lengthy church ceremony. The exchange of food again marks Christmas day, and we appreciate the yams, pineapple, and cake-like sweets that we receive in return for noodles with tinned peas and tobacco. We, too, try to bake some simple pancakes to share but realise that we have to sieve all our flour through a mosquito net, hoping that this catches the beetles inside. It is not the first time we have struggled with critters infesting our flour. We have eaten our pancakes with closed eyes several times before, hoping that not too many beetles have escaped our improvised sieve.

During these last few weeks on Niuafo'ou, we collect as many observations on the Malau as possible. Our marking of the birds on Motu Molemole is almost complete—we now know how many pairs live there. Also, we discover that only the birds living on this islet seem to lay eggs there, meaning no Malau females from outside territories fly in to use the local laying burrows. We also find that they produce eggs all year round, meaning there is no distinctive breeding season. After counting all the eggs laid over a certain period, we can estimate how many eggs each pair produces, which is crucial base information for conservation. We find that the pairs deposit a new egg approximately every 15 days, and if you calculate this over a whole year, it is evident that they can lay about 24 eggs a year, more than most other birds.

A clutch size describes the number of eggs at a single brooding event, usually within one nest. Birds that sit on their eggs to incubate them are limited in their clutch size by how many eggs they can cover with their body and how many chicks they can afterwards feed and protect. Together with other environmental and developmental factors, these restrictions explain why most songbirds only lay 2-5 eggs, and the maximum number of eggs known per clutch is 18 (in some partridges)[1]. Malau and other megapodes can produce more offspring, mainly because they are not limited by the usual restrictions. They don't have to sit on eggs or provide parental care, so they are only limited by the amount of protein-rich food they can find while producing an egg. For them, it makes sense to produce many offspring, as the mortality of chicks is generally higher when parents don't look after them.

As a woman, I especially admire the female Malau. We compare the average weight of the females we caught with the average weight of the eggs we found, and it is evident that the egg weighs about 24% of the female's body. This proportion would be equivalent to a 60 kg woman giving birth to a 14.4 kg child—ouch! And they don't just do this once or every few years like us humans, but approximately every 15 days. The heavy egg also explains why we don't see birds from outside the islet fly to Motu Molemole for egg-laying. They don't seem to try to fly with such a heavy load. In addition, they depend on their partner to help them find enough protein to produce such a large egg. The male defends a territory where they, and no other Malau, feed on what they can find, and he occasionally even holds up food items for her. Let's hope the males don't cheat!

Laying such a large egg with lots of yolk is the only investment the female makes into her offspring, as she does not look after them after hatching. A large egg can produce a strong, independent chick, and a lot of yolk means the chick has a lunch packet available for a prolonged stay of 60 or more days inside the egg and the first hours after hatching. The little chicks don't use up all the yolk during incubation but suck some of it into their belly before hatching. What fascinating adaptations to a highly unusual approach to incubation and hatching!

During our weeks at Motu Molemole, only interrupted by the weekend trips to Esia, we are surprised again by how quiet it can be on an islet on the lake on the island. Our background noises are the gentle waves of the crater lake hitting the shoreline, the wind blowing in the casuarina trees, and the occasional fruit dove or Malau calling. Occasionally, locals walk along the crater rim and call down our names: Ana e Ivo Malau! Otherwise, there is not much else to stimulate the senses. After dark, we are so desperate for entertainment that we keep re-reading Werner's three National Geographic magazines. We also listen to the songs on our two tapes so often that we might suffer from earworms for the rest of our lives. I think songs like 'You Might Think I'm Crazy' by The Cars and 'In the Midnight Hour' by The Commitments will stay with me forever. Another interesting side effect of having so few distractions is that my mind is starting to remember things

---

1. https://web.stanford.edu/group/stanfordbirds/text/essays/Variation_in_Clutch.html

from the past that I have never thought about before. For example, which petrol station I went to with my grandmother when I was six years old. A psychologist would have a ball studying the crazy effect of quietness on one's mind here on this islet.

After our quiet weeks in the crater, we don't mind our Sunday returns to the village and chats with the locals, especially Kailao. Somehow, though, I am less and less willing to talk about local politics, Ofato, how fat or not fat we are, and when the next ship may arrive. My mind is starting to wander into the future, to a future back home. Maybe it is homesickness; perhaps I have concluded that while we tried so hard to be accepted by the locals, we will always be pālangi who do not quite fit in. And I now wonder how much I want to fit in. My patience for everyday 'issues' has decreased. I am less tolerant of the type of conversations we have with the locals, the heat, the deterioration of our equipment, and the mini beasts that invade our lives.

We weren't surprised to find beetles in our rice and flour, which is expected here, but not in the treasured spaghetti Rolf gave us! These tiny weevil borers have created hollow spaghetti by gnawing through the centre, from one end to the other, without breaking the long noodles. All we can do again is cook the spaghetti and then fish out most of the beetles with a sieve. The combined effect of all these issues causes me to be quite moody, and poor Ivo is busy cheering me up. He is still more tolerant of such everyday affairs but is occasionally more depressed and pensive about our disagreements with Mr Hopps. At such times, I have to cheer him up. We make an excellent cheering team, and it looks like overall, our island test in living together is going well.

With many results on the Malau in our notebooks, we feel it is justified to fulfil a dream of Ivo's that is not related to our work: to find the old hiking path that takes you all around the island along the 200-metre high rim of the crater. We had read about it in old accounts written when white people visited the island more often for copra production. At that time, locals established this path to harvest the copra produced in large amounts and sold to the main island for good money. Now, with copra trading almost dead, the locals don't have a reason to walk around the rim. Instead, they travel along the island road that lies on the outer slope of the crater, and they are not interested in using the overgrown rim path, even though it offers fantastic views over the island. Views are a tourist thing. Our search takes many hours, lots of bush bashing with the machete, and good practice in standing still when the hornets attack. We are rewarded with amazing views and the feeling of being natural explorers. Before returning in the late afternoon, the caldera with its lake and islets is bathed in a crimson twilight, and we can't help but think that this is one of the most beautiful views in the world.

We are spending our last few weeks on Niuafo'ou, and there is a lot of research on the Malau left to do. But unfortunately, my health deteriorates. My limbs and lip sometimes swell up overnight, and I suffer from strange rashes. Worse still are the abdominal pains that I have already suffered from periodically during these last few months. In particular, eating fatty food in the village seems to aggravate these, and I often have to decline the food cooked by Malohi's family. Dry crackers, breadfruit, and oats are what I mainly live on. It is time to catch that plane back home, have this checked out, and return to the diet I am more used to. Let's hope that the scheduled aircraft will indeed depart from Niuafo'ou in five weeks. For now, though, all that passes in our direction is a storm, a powerful storm indeed.

While this part of the South Pacific has very humid but stable weather for half the year, the other half is occupied by cyclones, also known as hurricanes to some. From November to about April, the islands can expect to be battered by two or three cyclones, and quite frequently, these are rather devastating. For us, it all starts with a stronger-than-usual wind while we spend a Sunday in Esia. While we are sitting on the doorstep of our hut, one of the gusts suddenly de-anchors the corrugated iron that surrounds our outhouse toilet, and the whole thing comes flying down the hill towards our house. In shock, we watch this corrugated rocket coming our way. My brain just thinks this can't be true, but Ivo's reflexes are quicker, and he shouts at me to jump inside and close the door. We manage to escape just in time while the toilet bomb roars past our entry and comes to rest not far away. The bachelors next door are bedazzled too. Even these usually cheerful men don't laugh about what just happened. Maybe they now understand that it would have been better if the outhouse had been anchored in the ground and not just placed around the pit latrine like a child's building toy.

This incident alerts us to the dangers of being in Esia during a strong storm. There are too many loose things lying around that could become dangerous missiles when carried through the air. Too many sheets of corrugated iron and other items are capable of inflicting sudden decapitation. We prefer to be in the bush, where the danger of falling trees is more predictable. So off we head to Motu Molemole. We carry enough supplies for two weeks and our radio as a messenger of any news about the storm. While walking in a sustained downpour and watching the palm fronds fold in like umbrellas that have been blown inside out, we realise that this storm is strong indeed.

Rowing our dinghy through the high waves of the crater lake to Motu Molemole is hard work, and we are exhausted when we arrive at camp. Luckily, we know how to start a fire for cooking in the constant rain, even though it means using some of our precious fuel supplies. We have yet to experience how much noise wind can make, noise that can drive you crazy. The wind experiences friction while passing through the many thousands of thin needle-like leaves on the casuarina trees around us, amplifying the howling to a roar. There is nowhere to hide from this intense noise, and we become moody and tense.

Over the next few days, the air becomes uncomfortably humid and sticky, a likely precursor to a storm. After that, everything becomes damp and starting a fire is a monstrous chore. We now agree with what we have read in one of Werner's National Geographic magazines about cyclones. Humans give them names as this kind of personifies this incomprehensible force that comes towards them. It helps you believe that the storm is more transparent, maybe more under control. 'Our' storm is called 'Kina', and our jaws drop when we hear on the radio that it has already caused widespread destruction in Fiji and is now moving at 200 km/h eastwards, directly towards us.

I go into panic mode, ready to pack everything we need and spend the night in our little dinghy on the small crater lake on Motu Molemole. The lake is our emergency destination should the cyclone hit, as it is pretty sheltered by the surrounding crater rim, and we would be less likely to get hit by trees. Ivo keeps calm, even jokes about how, if the cyclone hits, we might receive some care packages from the Tongan government. The wind has completely stopped now; it is literally the calm before the storm. An eerie atmosphere lies in the air, even all the birds have stopped singing, and the only noise comes from our radio. We first try our luck with Radio Tonga, but they only mention the threat to the larger islands in the south, as if Niuafo'ou didn't exist. Radio New Zealand is more thorough, and we are so grateful that they at least acknowledge our tiny speck in the ocean. As howling, gloomy darkness descends, we are glued to our Sony World Receiver. Time melts in fatigue. In our trusty tent, the rain, thunder, and darkness all seem to merge.

Towards the morning, Radio New Zealand informs us that we were rather lucky last night. Not one storm moved close by, but two. Niuafo'ou was wedged between 'Kina' and 'Tina'. 'Kina' has changed direction and is moving towards Tongatapu. 'Tina' seems to be on its way to Samoa, and it was this storm whose outliers we experienced last night. The adventure is not over yet, though. Soon after, 'Nina' appears in the news. We find it hard to keep track of which of these similar-sounding storms is where, and as non-seafarers from the heart of Europe, we have no idea how strong one knot is. Maybe that's good for our nerves, though, because it means nothing to us when we hear that ferocious 'Nina' blows towards our island with a strength of 60 knots. Luckily, we don't know that this can be translated into a 'violent storm' that can cause 'considerable structural damage'.

We can no longer receive Radio New Zealand; the transmission is not strong enough. Without this lifeline to news, we have to revert to the weak reception of Radio Tonga again. In the middle of the following night, Ivo climbs the crater rim of Motu Molemole in the copious rain, hoping to get a stronger signal. Intermittently, he hears bits of news, mainly about Nina heading from Tuvalu towards Samoa, which is pretty close to us. This news doesn't alleviate our fears as we don't know whether this means it won't hit us or whether we are just too small to be mentioned. The following morning, we conclude that the eye of 'Nina' has kindly passed our island 60 miles to the northwest. We got away with her little toe and two sleepless nights. Our friends in Esia are all ok too, except that debris is lying everywhere. The people on Tongatapu were less lucky. Buildings were destroyed, four ships sank, and the locals had no food and light for two days. Unfortunately, 'Nina' visited on a Sunday, when the shops were closed as they always are on a Sunday. Germans would probably have stocked up on supplies before the weekend, especially because days ago, it was already evident that these storms were heading towards Tonga. The radio reported them originating near Northern Australia more than a week ago. But most Tongans did not stock up and were thus starving when the cyclones arrived on a Sunday.

28

A Bit Less Pālangi?

Malohi and his family now repeatedly tell us that we are the good pālangi. They praise us for being good in Anga Faka-Tongá, the Tongan way of life, and that many people on the island know this. This indicates they think we are a bit more Tongan, hence less pālangi, and we are still coming to grips with this new status. First of all, this means they expect us to share what we have with our fellow islanders. In Tonga, if you have more than others, you need to share. Kailao's and Malohi's families have, by now, accepted that we want food in return for what we give them, but many others are not aware of this trading deal and seem to think that if we are less pālangi, we also need to share more. Accordingly, more people than ever ask for tobacco, and we might soon start dreaming about people asking us constantly, *"toi pe tapaka?"*—"do you have tobacco?"

It might not just be our status as less pālangi that encourages people to ask for things, but also the locals' experience with the missionaries from the many different churches established on this island since the 1800s. The clerics have always given the locals all kinds of goods as a reward for attending church, particularly the Methodists with their Free Wesleyan Church or the Catholics with their Catholic Mission church. There are also smaller churches, such as the Mormon church and the Church of Jesus Christ of Latter-day Saints. Every person identifies with some sort of Christianity on this island.

And even though we are not missionaries, we are still white people who, to many locals, may have a similar 'giving attitude'.

The young men, in particular, are becoming bolder and bolder towards us, ignoring Kailao's order to leave us alone. Thrice, different groups of teenagers visit us on Motu Molemole, and each time we fear the implications for the Malau and our research. The teens ask for tobacco and corned beef, and when we say no, they leave to dig out some Malau eggs and hunt the adults. If we gave in to their demands, they would come again and tell all their friends to visit us too, so we can only try to talk to them and explain why the Malau needs to be protected. We are up against some high levels of testosterone and youngsters who just want to have fun. One of them even writes a message to us in the sand next to a laying burrow: *Tapu!*—Taboo! He obviously refers to the ancient concept of tapu, which was very important in all Polynesian societies before Christianity arrived. This concept referred to anything that was forbidden due to sacredness. The young man who wrote the note has just dug out some eggs himself, so this activity can't be that taboo!

When we ask Kailao for advice, he comes back with a piece of thin wood on which he has written in Tongan: "Careful, eggs poisoned." We are to install this sign next to the main Malau laying burrow on Motu Molemole. Kailao doesn't think that explaining anything about conservation to the teens would stop them from digging for eggs, but this would. And indeed, he is right. Next time they visit, after reading the sign, the young men leave us alone, at least for now.

One Sunday, only one, we are naughty and don't both return to the village for church. We are amid some exciting observations of the Malau at the egg-laying burrow and don't want to miss out on this. Instead, Ivo walks back to the village on Saturday and tells Malohi that I have injured my leg and can't walk. Lying is not what we usually do, but there is no other excuse Malohi would accept for not coming to church. Upon hearing this news, both Malohi and Kailao present Ivo with roots to take back to Motu Molemole, and Malohi asks Ivo to meet at the edge of the crater lake on Sunday. That day, we are moved to tears when Malohi walks down the steep path to the lake to deliver three loaves of bread to Ivo. For the first time, he presents us with more food than the weekly allowance we are paying for and some food that we usually never receive. Yes, we have paid for a whole drum of fuel for his tractor, and yes, we have promised him a watch that we have brought back from Vava'u, but at that moment, we feel that his gift is a sharing and caring gift, not just an exchange of goods. This does leave us very moved indeed.

Apart from food, we now also need to get news from the locals. Our little radio has died, exhausted from the frequent use during the cyclone event. Kailao helps us out by lending us the newspapers he received with the last plane. They are a few weeks old but better than nothing. Somehow, though, the world out there seems very far away on this distant island. We read with limited interest that Bill Clinton has been elected president of the US. There is a war in Somalia, and in former East Germany, neo-Nazis have vandalised whole towns while onlookers sadly cheer them on. To us, though, the more critical news focuses on the arrival of the next plane and whether any cyclones might interfere with that momentous event.

29

Stuck on Tin Can Island?

A trip with our dinghy to the shores of the crater lake ends with bad news. We accidentally discover Lakepi, who is sitting on a rock, fishing for Tilapia. At first, we do not see him because his dark skin and brown shorts make him blend in with his surroundings and somewhat camouflage him. We only notice him when we get close, and our brains have little time to adjust to the torrent of words he immediately throws at us. All we understand are the Tongan words for: aeroplane/year/not/this. We ask him several times to repeat this more slowly until we realise that he is not joking and that this news is likely accurate. There will be no more plane coming this year. Most likely, Lakepi is waiting for any sign from us that we are desperate to leave the island, a sign that would fuel the gossip that we do not like it here. Gathering our greatest self-discipline, we keep our expressions neutral and joke with him instead: "*Kovi vakapuna!*"—"Naughty aeroplane!" Lakepi cannot convey any details, Ivo needs to stay on Motu Molemole to finish recording the Malau, so I venture into Esia to find out more. At first, I have to calm down Malohi, who is upset that I, as a woman, have walked through the bush on my own. I reassure him that the *tevolo* will not hurt me and that we need to find out more about this plane business. It is Kailao who knows the whole story. Apparently, the coconut palms along the runway have grown too tall and obscure the sight for the pilots, so they cannot land.

There are many palms, and nobody has ever cut them. We doubt that they ever will be felled, and we strongly suspect that this is just an excuse for Royal Tongan Airline to save some money.

We have five weeks left before our flight back to Germany from Nuku'alofa. It is not a lot of time when you are stuck on an island, and the only hope of getting away has been reduced to the slight possibility of a ship arriving sometime before then. Kailao thinks there might be a chance of this happening. At least a vessel would give us the option of taking home more of our equipment than a plane, but we cannot take much of it anyway. In his letters, the Professor insists that we leave most of it behind because he will find someone else to take over our project, so we will store the equipment with Malohi and Kailao instead. The sponsors have paid for it, and the Professor is the official person on the sponsor letters, so he has to decide this. Plus, Ivo still wants to complete his degree with him. It is better not to annoy the professor anymore since we are already in his bad books for leaving earlier.

Being deprived of our best chance to leave the island in time somehow also saps our energy. Disappointed and frustrated, we sit in our dinghy and drift around on the crater lake, aimlessly and wherever the wind takes us, unwilling to face the mosquitos in the bush, unprepared to make a fire and cook some breadfruit and corned beef, and definitely unready to think of the possibility that we might have to stay on this island quite a bit longer than planned.

Once we have gathered enough energy to row back and head to the village, the latest gossip awaits us: a ship will arrive in two weeks. This news revives us. Knowing that our departure is hopefully imminent, we work hard to complete the estimate of how many Malau inhabit the whole island. Our outboard engine, essential for our work, breaks down mid-way on a trip, and we spend several hours pulling it all apart to get to the leaking seal of the carburetor. Thankfully, Ivo knows enough about engines to somehow put all the little bits and pieces that we have cleaned back where they belong. Without the engine, we would not reach the more remote parts of the island to count the Malau. Also, rowing in the crater lake against the wind would exhaust us. We already lose time and energy every time our dinghy leaks, and one of us has to constantly scoop out the water while the other operates the engine.

The last day of 1992 arrives. We celebrate another New Year's eve on Motu Molemole, drawing another happy piglet on each other's bellies, and making another big fire to commemorate the event. Our supplies of cookies or wine are exhausted, but we have each other and agree that the 'island test' has gone well so far. Of course, there are times when the circumstances take the laughter from our faces, but we mostly manage to find things to joke about and cheer each other up. Our conversations are the best way to escape from the island in our minds, and lately, they have ventured a lot into the other world out there, the world back home.

Our trips to different parts of the island often leave us so exhausted that we do not talk much afterwards and just collapse onto our camping mats in the tent. On these trips, we usually land with our boat in impenetrable vegetation, then venture into the bush to play the calls of the Malau and record how many respond. This data will form the basis for our overall estimate of the population size. Authorities will need this estimate to assess the Malau's conservation status, and this assessment will determine how much money flows into its future conservation.

We also measure the vegetation density to link this to the Malau density. Such observations will help determine whether conservation measures should focus on areas with a particular type and density of plants. All of this drains us, especially in the current climate. The heat and humidity seem to have increased threefold, and while our sweat glands are working in overdrive, we gulp down as many mineral tablets as possible. Our shirts do not even smell anymore as our sweat seems to be pure water. Or maybe we have simply lost our sense of smell.

While waiting for the ship, we come across an educational paragraph in our book about Tongan culture that we should have read months ago: "It is very common for Tongans to arrive late for social events. Being late does not necessarily indicate that the activity is not perceived as important. Rather, punctuality is less important. Tongans prefer to enjoy the present moment and take their time. 'Tongan Time' is a common expression that captures the Tongan laid-back approach to time-keeping." We have experienced this many times, and we wish that, at least this time, the promised ship will be punctual and that we will be able to catch our flight back home.

Full of hope, we pack up our camp on Motu Molemole. Being careful not to leave anything behind, we burn some leftovers and stuff everything else into our dinghy. This loyal friend is now leaking so badly that it has just enough air left to get us to the other side of the crater lake. We say goodbye to this islet that has been our second home for so long while one of us scoops out the water, and the other holds on to equipment and steering rod. It takes several trips to return everything to Esia. I feel weak as my gut issues have worsened again, but I am convinced that I will get better once my food is no longer a nutritional chore but a choice of options that I currently lack on this island.

Gossip now says that the ship will arrive next week. Malohi insists it will come on Thursday, i.e., in three days. Fortunately, we also ask the local teacher. According to the radio, a vessel of an unknown name will depart the main island on Thursday, and hence will arrive here two or three days later. The teacher is also hoping to leave with us. For Malohi and others, it doesn't matter that it will take at least two days for the ship to make its way up here—Thursday is close enough if you live on Tongan Time. On Friday, we start packing before visiting Laione for the last time. He is cheerful and happy as usual; we talk about this and that until he casually mentions towards the end of our stay that the vessel we are waiting for is broken and can't be repaired. His information also comes from the radio. Apparently, the ship hit a reef while approaching the main island. Our only consolation is that this vessel is the *Fokololo-oe Hau*, the "swimming coffin." Maybe it is fate that we weren't meant to travel on that one. Then, Laione casually mentions that a large cruise ship is anchored off this island's shore today.

Amidst our disappointment, our thoughts race. Would we be able to pack up everything quickly enough, say goodbye, and somehow get to the cruise ship, hoping that they would rescue two poor, stranded researchers? Unlikely, unfortunately. If only we had known earlier, but our expedition clothes would probably not live up to the dress standard on that luxury cruise anyway. The teacher later confirms that this last hope of departing has already departed. It is one of those cruise liners that occasionally visit the island so passengers can post their mail—not to send a speedy message to someone, but to send unique stamps that read "Niuafo'ou" or "Tin Can Island" instead of "Tonga" as the country of origin.

We couldn't care less about stamps right now; all we want is to get home. There is one more glimmer of hope. The teacher mentions that the Tongan military will send one of their three boats. These boats occasionally show up near the island to survey the outer borders of Tonga and deter foreign fishing fleets. When they come up here, they usually anchor off the island for a few days, chat with the local chiefs, and hand out tobacco to some lucky men. Unfortunately, travelling on that vessel is not permitted, except for two high-ranking locals who have managed to secure a spot because they urgently need to leave for the main island.

We are obviously not high-ranking enough to be accepted on those grounds, but we also know how far money can take you in Tonga. Some would call it bribery. Not that we are rich, but we have some funds left, and things don't cost a lot in Tonga compared to back home. The Tongan military would, of course, never accept bribery, but they may welcome a donation to support the excellent work they are doing. With this plan in mind, we approach the one soldier who serves as a local contact for the military on the island. The locals call him *tamasi'i shatia*, the "boy soldier." It amuses us how they often incorporate new words into their language, such as *shatia* for soldier. The shatia's information is slightly vague: Yes, there will be a military boat coming sometime within the next week, and yes, we might be able to get onto that boat with a donation if we ask the captain upon its arrival.

It's waiting time again. Our nerves are frayed, and we find it more than challenging to maintain our enthusiasm for being here. Nobody knows exactly when the military will arrive, so we can't venture to the refreshing lake or elsewhere away from Esia. Stuck in our partly disintegrated hut, we endure the mould that has grown on everything, the suffocating humidity and buzzing minibeasts, more breadfruit and cooking bananas, and the uncertainty of whether we will be able to leave.

One highlight is that Ivo has managed to repair our world receiver radio. The German radio—*Deutsche Welle*—broadcasts a four-hour-long programme every day, and we often listen to that same programme with news and songs from home, two or three times in a row. Sometimes we have to laugh at ourselves when we realise that we are just lying there for hours, listening to the radio, staring at our fingernails, and trying not to move in the heat. Our thoughts repeatedly seem to circle around the same things, predominantly our arguments with Mr Hopps, and about the Professor's inability to call this project quits so that we can't officially leave our equipment with the locals. Ivo still has the energy to occasionally talk to Malohi about all the local Tongan names for plants and places on the island. Malohi is very impressed by his interest. I stay hidden in our hut, partly because my gut issues are rather debilitating. If it weren't for Ivo's support, I would become quite depressed. Is this what island fever feels like? I'm not sure, but what I do know is that we will try every possible avenue to get onto that military ship.

Finally, we receive news from the teacher that the ship will arrive early tomorrow. We are reasonably confident that his interpretation of time is not guided by Tongan Time, and we pack up the few things that we can take without them becoming a burden. The last thing we want is for the captain to reject us because we have too much stuff. The most valuable luggage in our barrels is the pile of notebooks with all our observations of the Malau, but we also pack our trusted little radio, manual camera with all the films that still need developing, Walkman with recordings of Malau songs, a tin of corned beef, and a few hand-woven fans as mementoes of Niuafo'ou. We include the compass on top, just in case the soldiers on that boat use unreliable navigation methods like other captains we have travelled with. Our last conversations with Malohi are light-hearted on the outside but overshadowed by deep sadness inside us. We can't convey to him why we are so desperate to leave for good without hurting his pride.

Most of our clothes, leftover food, tarps, boxes, tools, and other smaller equipment will stay in the hut for Malohi to use once we have told him that we won't be returning. The solar cells, battery, and attached light are going to Kailao. His five school-aged children will benefit from being able to study under light after dark. Our last conversations with Kailao are not at all light-hearted. He is reticent, presumably to hide his emotions, and we struggle to find the words that could bridge the widening gap between us. At midnight, he comes to our house and secretly picks up the solar equipment, hoping that Malohi's family won't notice. If we do manage to leave, and once we have obtained official permission from the Professor to hand over our equipment, he will be able to utilise it. We don't care whether he uses it beforehand; we expect he will. Apart from being disturbed by Kailao, our hopefully last night on Niuafo'ou is made sleepless by our growing excitement and the humidity, which seems worse than ever. Maybe our endurance level has just sunk more than ever, especially mine.

30

Almost Killed by the King

At first light, we join Malohi and many others on the tractor's trailer to head to the 'harbour' at Futu where the military boat will arrive. While driving past the thousands of coconut palms, black lava fields, and bright blue sea, I notice that I can no longer appreciate where I am. Instead, I am jaded by my surroundings. Symptom: A complete lack of enthusiasm for where I am. Diagnosis: Island fever. All I want is to leave, no matter how hard I try to suppress this feeling. I especially try to hide this emotion in front of Ivo in case we can't get onto that military boat and have to stay a few more weeks or months longer. His attitude is a bit more laid-back, which is probably a better approach to dealing with uncertainties.

Many men cover the rock platform at the harbour, sitting cross-legged, a bit like crabs waiting for the tide to come in, except that they are waiting for tobacco. Malohi joins them, and we will remember the last picture of this proud man sitting among others in his blue working overalls and straw hat, hoping to get hold of enough tobacco and paper for a cigarette or two. Kailao, on the other hand, does not join the crowd on the platform. His social status as a policeman allows him to join the few standing men at the tip of the platform, closest to the sea. When the first dinghy returns from the ship anchored far out at sea, he manages to secure enough tobacco for a miniature cigarette, then paces up and down between the people like a tiger. He ignores us, most likely to avoid fuelling any rumours about his close relationship with us, and I feel quite sad about that.

We push through the crowds to reach the end of the platform, and suddenly, events unfold quickly. The dinghy heading for the ship is about to leave with the teacher and several other people in it, and there is only space for one more person. I push Ivo to jump in, as a woman can't appear in front of the captain by herself. Ivo is not the most confident and assertive person, and I usually love him for it, but not today. Once aboard the ship, he and the teacher talk to the captain, but the captain completely ignores Ivo and only talks to the teacher in rapid Tongan that is hard to understand. Ivo feels so disheartened and stressed that he forgets to offer our bribe in time, and the audience with the captain is over before he gets a chance to do so. The teacher translates to Ivo that he has been accepted because the local soldier boy has booked him in, but not us. We are only allowed to come along if no other Tongans want to join by 4 pm. The captain's decision most likely means no—a no to pālangis—as the platform is full of Tongans who hope to leave. Some are school-aged children who go to school on the main island, and others need to visit sick or dying relatives on other islands.

There aren't the right words to describe my disappointment and growing anger at Ivo for not being more assertive. Poor Ivo, he doesn't deserve my moods, but the thought of staying on this island any longer seems unacceptable at that very moment. A severe case of island fever. Slowly, very slowly, we start summoning some energy by scraping together the good things we can still do, now that we most likely need to stay longer. For example, exploring certain beautiful landscapes on the island and harvesting the tomatoes that I have grown outside our hut.

Close to 4 pm, we both grab a spot in the dinghy and return to the ship. This time, I take over the conversation. In the torrent of words that I throw at the captain, I plead for his help, and I don't forget to diplomatically include the donation of 250 Pa'anga if he takes us to the main island, or 100 Pa'anga if we can at least travel to Vava'u. Finally, in a very authoritative voice, the captain asks me how much luggage we have, and I downplay it by responding that two little bags are waiting for us ashore. Theoretically, you could call our backpack barrels a bag. "You can bring it," he says. Did I misunderstand him? I have to ask again, but yes, it is true, we can come along to Vava'u. What a huge relief, enormous indeed! While not yet near the international airport, Vava'u is better than being stuck here, and we should be able to catch a flight from Vava'u to Nuku'alofa just in time for our departure to Germany.

We take a last trip in the dinghy back ashore to fetch our luggage. A final goodbye to Malohi, after we have informed him, to his apparent surprise, that we did manage to get onto the boat. If this were an official goodbye forever, there would traditionally be the need to wallow in tears, to have a big feast, and our obvious joy at being able to leave would hurt Malohi's pride. But there is no time for any of this. All that Malohi says is "*Sai pe*"—"that's ok"—thus giving his blessing for us to leave. If only we could express to Malohi that we are sorry for not always having lived up to his expectations of how people in his care should behave, especially me as a woman. If only we could thank him properly for all the good laughs and conversations together and for the many lessons he has given us on traditional customs, language, and culture. But there is only time for a simple "*malo'aupito*"—"thank you very much"—before we need to rush to gather our belongings and head back to the ship. Kailao is nowhere to be seen, and so, to our dismay, we can't even say goodbye to him at all.

Back on the 30-metre-long vessel, we would prefer to join the teacher and the two other locals who secured a lift, but we have to meet the scary captain in the mess deck and hand over our voluntary donation of 100 Pa'anga. The mess usually serves as the soldiers' common room. It contains a shiny table with a comfy bench, a narrow floor space, and three large, framed portraits of the Tongan monarchs on the wall. To our surprise, when it is just the three of us, the 35-year-old captain drops his authoritative demeanour, becomes quite approachable, and enjoys a good chat. He orders me to sleep in the mess, as he doesn't have any dedicated cabins for ladies, whereas Ivo is to join the other men in one large area under the deck. The anchor is lifted soon after, and the first few minutes of travelling already reveal how rough the sea is today. The relatively small boat rolls about in unpredictable ways. Ivo is already feeling so sick that he cannot fathom making his way down under deck. I am sitting upright, determined not to let seasickness dampen my newly found spirits, but after an hour, I too join Ivo in the horizontal position on the floor of our makeshift cabin.

During the following hours, we reassure each other that we have never felt so sick before. The boat constantly tilts about 45 degrees to either side and hits the waves with loud bangs, followed by a discordant creaking. For quite a while, we contemplate how we should make it to the toilet, which is luckily only 10 metres away, and eventually, this becomes our most significant achievement of the night. Finally, the second officer in charge kindly brings us some bedding to sleep on, walking steadily on his feet as if there were no waves at all. We try to spread out the bedding, but it is impossible, and we end up wrapped up in blankets like a sausage in a roll, falling into an exhausted semi-dormant state with vivid dreams about rollercoasters.

Suddenly, Ivo wakes me first with a loud yell, then laconically declares that the King has hit him but luckily has not killed him. He does have a bloody lip and bruised cheeks, though. A closer inspection of the wall above our makeshift bed reveals the cause and shows that his interpretation of the situation is incorrect. The portrait of the Crown

Prince of Tonga, not the King, has fallen and hit Ivo on the face. An even closer inspection reveals how lucky he was: The Crown Prince's painting is much smaller than that of the Tongan King, which hangs right next to it, with a much heavier wooden frame, and also dangles precariously loose. If the King had fallen onto Ivo, the captain might have been in a difficult situation, having to explain why a pālangi was killed in his mess while asleep with his wife on a ship supposed to transport Tongan soldiers only. Nevertheless, for now, we dare to take the King off the wall, hoping that we will be forgiven for this rebellious act, as Tongans do maintain a quaint reverence for all things monarchy.

Due to the weather, the ship travels at such a low speed, 14 km/h, that it takes us 14 hours to cover the 200 km to our first destination: Niuatoputapu. This island to the east is regarded as our island's sister. The two are called the Niuas, but the siblings are of different parentage. While Niuafo'ou is purebred volcanic, Niuatoputapu has mixed volcanic and coral features. We have read about this island's fame among archaeologists, based on excavations that uncovered numerous sherds of ancient pottery. These are seen as proof that about 3,000 years ago, the Lapita people inhabited this island. They were the first people to sail to Polynesia, demonstrating fantastic navigation skills. While travelling, they left a unique trail of decorative pottery on many islands between the Bismarck Archipelago and Tonga.

Today, though, the people on Niuatoputapu don't seem very different from those on Niuafo'ou. Our vessel stays anchored for one day and one night, and we are asked to leave during the day. The stable, non-moving ground gives us a chance to feel human again. It doesn't take long for the rumour to go around: "*Ana e Ivo Malau kuo a'u mai*"—"Ann and Ivo Malau have arrived." We didn't think we were that famous, but obviously, our neighbours knew about our existence. "*Toi pe tapaka?*" No, sorry, no tobacco left. Not much left at all, only our last tin of corned beef. A friendly lady named Laveni approaches us, and we ask her whether we can pay her to cook us some roots to go with the tin. She apologises for only having breadfruit available. This food choice is nothing new to us, and we agree with her menu, as our stomachs need some sustenance after last night. Laveni even runs to the shop to buy a packet of two-minute noodles for us. The local shop stocks such unique delicacies because Royal Tongan Airline flies here more often. So there is a difference to Niuafo'ou at last. The thousands of coconut palms are no different, though, nor is the high humidity or the number of mosquitos. After our frugal meal, we find an area with a bit of a breeze, sleep under some coconut palms, nearly get hit by a falling coconut, and desperately await the time when we are allowed back on the ship.

Onboard, we can't recall having slept that well for months. After a refreshing shower, a nice meal with the second officer, and a chat over coffee with the captain, we drift into a sleep of exhaustion while kept cool by the air conditioning unit in our mess.

Meanwhile, the ship is safely anchored in calm waters. We are grateful to the Australian government for donating this boat to Tonga. "We got it as part of the Pacific Class Patrol Boat programme," the captain tells us, "and it's really well equipped for travelling in the Pacific." That's a relief and probably the only large boat in Tonga that can claim this adaptation to ocean travelling! Over breakfast with the crew, we realise that these young soldiers are cheerful, like many young Tongan men we've met before—lots of joking, laughing, and singing. The main difference is that they speak good English and have landed a dream job with a regular salary that probably supports their family. They tell us that Australia has donated the ship because it wants Tonga to safeguard its border against potential invaders from the east.

One of the soldiers asks us whether we know Heinz, who also lives in Germany. He has recently met him here in Tonga. To a Tongan, it is hard to imagine that Germany is slightly larger than the island they come from and that we don't know everyone in our home territory, whereas they do. It is not the first time a Tongan has asked us whether we know someone from Germany. "Sorry," we say, "we don't know Heinz, but we can look out for him."

It would be nice to pretend that we could relax in our mess a bit longer, but 300 kilometres are waiting to be covered, again over an angry, windswept sea. So for the next 14 hours, we give up on sitting upright again and desperately think of things to focus on while battling the need to throw up. At Neiafu in Vava'u, we are so grateful to hear the sound of the anchor rattling, and we thank the captain and his crew for their outstanding hospitality and kindness. They haven't even complained about our removal of the King from the wall!

Back at the Hilltop Guesthouse, exhaustion stops us from answering many of Rolf's worried questions about our well-being, but we gratefully accept the soup he serves. Our bones and muscles don't want to lie flat anymore, but our brains and stomachs need rest. So my last thought before falling asleep is that we are finally here, that from now on, we will always sleep in a proper bed on proper solid ground, away from centipedes, waves, and corned beef.

It is January 1993, and we have one week left before our international departure from Nuku'alofa. One last island hop to organise, but this should be easy given that Royal Tongan Airline flies back and forth between Vava'u and the main island daily. Or so we think. All flights are booked out, we are told. There is no way we will give up now that we have successfully managed the previous big island hop. We will not be stuck on Vava'u after avoiding getting marooned on Niuafo'ou. Option one is to board another corroded ferry that is supposed to leave for the main island the next day. But travelling in Tongan Time again is too risky, and the thought of setting foot on a boat for two days once more is too unbearable. Option two involves our friend Rolf and two friendly young German tourists staying in his guest house. Using his great convincing skills, Rolf persuades them to trade in their tickets for the next day in return for new tickets valid for the week after. They don't mind staying on Vava'u a bit longer than on Tongatapu, as this island group has more to offer in tourist terms. They are also fascinated by our stories and make us think that maybe one day, I should turn these adventures, meticulously documented in my letters, into a book.

One last fax from the Professor also awaits us in Vava'u, and it almost blows us off our feet. He now wants us to revisit Late Island to check how many Malau eggs have hatched, as he wants to keep promoting the success of the translocation. Our description of the hardships involved in getting there does not seem to have impressed him. We are confident that this is the last thing we want to do now, and we don't care about his lack of understanding anymore. The only trips we are still willing to do are south to Nuku'alofa and then west to Europe.

After a sad goodbye from Rolf and Lautoka, we arrive in Nuku'alofa without further complications. There is one last thing we want to do here before boarding the plane to Europe. During the previous 17 months, we have consumed about eight large 10-litre buckets full of 'Pacific Cracker Biscuits'. These are plain squares that contain mainly flour and water and are so dry that saliva alone is not enough to wash them down. We would call a concoction like this a dry cracker at home, but here it is declared a biscuit. With their colourful tropical label, featuring hibiscus flowers, palm trees, and deliciously prepared crackers, these buckets were often our only go-to when we were short of food, or my stomach was too upset to accept anything else. To honour them, we request to visit the biscuit factory, and the employees of the Sitani Mafi & Co bakery are happy to show us around.

The production of the island biscuits partly explains their taste—a sizeable tube-like structure of metal towers in a dust-filled hall where breathing would require a mask. No masks can be seen here. The structure reminds me of one of those automatic carwash places, just smaller and rustier. A massive dough ball is inserted at one end, then flattened by a roll covered in brush-like spikes. The squeaking brush collects the dust from the air and then rolls it onto the dough while flattening the mixture into a thin layer. The second machine cuts it into squares before the assembly line moves these into a large oven to be baked. Ten women stand close together at the end of the line, packing the crackers into their buckets. In Germany, two people would suffice to do this job, but in Tonga, wages are cheap, and you always find more people employed. Some ladies have the final job of adding the colourful label to the buckets. This is the label that often left us mouth-watering and homesick on Niuafo'ou as it featured pictures of crackers topped with fresh tomatoes, cheese, and jam. Toppings we could only dream of on that island. One of the ladies hands us a label as a souvenir, and it will join the beautiful hand-woven fans that we were given on Niuafo'ou as the only material memories of our time in Tonga.

One last time, Tongan Time catches up to us when the Royal Tongan Airline flight to Fiji is first delayed by one day, and we then have to catch two planes to get there instead of one. One flight south to Auckland, another back north to Fiji. A useless detour, but at least we get to see the sweeping hills of New Zealand from the air, and we get served champagne twice. Luckily, we have some spare time in Fiji and eventually board the huge jumbo jet to Europe. Everything seems so vast to us after 17 months in Tonga, such as the seats, crowds of people, in-flight meals, and engine noise. It is overwhelming and makes us aware that somehow, we have changed. It will take us some time to adapt to a faster, noisier, and bigger lifestyle again. I am trying to find some sentimental goodbye words to write in the last letter to my parents, but my head seems empty. Emotions only start coming up when, many hours later, we see the map of Europe appearing on the plane's screen. It is almost too hard to believe that we are approaching that continent which we do call home, a continent that, in my thinking, has become such a far-away destination, separated by almost 10,000 km and a large stretch of sea. For now, I am tucking away the memories of Tonga in my brain, focusing on re-entering pālangi world again. But one day, I will dig them back out and proudly tell my kids, that's for sure.

Afterword: Back Home with Updates

As I am writing this book, 30 years later, Tonga is unfortunately featured in the news worldwide due to a violent volcanic eruption on 15 January 2022, which has caused fatalities and severe destruction all over the kingdom. A new volcano named Hunga Tonga—Hunga Ha'apai, about 60 km north of Tongatapu, erupted with such force that the resulting shockwave, devastating tsunami, and ash pollution have been described as a "one in a thousand years" event[1]. Sadly, three people lost their lives on other islands, but Niuafo'ou was relatively unaffected due to its remote location and high elevation. Only limited ash from the eruption may have reached the island, as satellite images detected ash only up to 30 km south of Niuafo'ou[2].

After the eruption, on 1 February 2022, the first cases of Covid-19 in Tonga were detected among port workers handling aid equipment sent as part of the recovery relief efforts[3]. Until then, Tonga had managed to stay Covid-free, but has since had to battle the pandemic by introducing lockdowns and increasing vaccination rates to the best of its abilities. In mid-April 2022, the lockdown was extended to the outer islands, including Niuafo'ou[4].

---

1. https://www.abc.net.au/news/2022-01-22/satellite-data-images-reveal-power-of-tonga-volcano-eruption/100773458

2. https://volcano.si.edu/volcano.cfm?vn=243040

3. https://matangitonga.to/2022/02/01/tonga-first-two-covid19-positive

4. https://matangitonga.to/2022/04/11/lockdown-extended-niuas-and-eua

In terms of volcanic activity on Niuafo'ou, we know that in 1999, when the volcanologist Paul Taylor visited, steam and volcanic gases (fumarolic activity) were observed in two areas of the inner crater. Gases were being released from a small field on the eastern shore of Vai Si'i. However, in 2002, activity seemed to have intensified around the lake's southern end (Vai Kona), with gases observed at several vents at Vai Si'i[5]. A 2022 summary of the island's geology describes it as a high-threat volcano for people to live on[6]. So, in summary, the volcano is still bubbling underneath, but no major eruptions have yet occurred, and the Malau can still use Niuafo'ou as an incubator for its eggs.

After returning home in 1993, we underwent routine health tests at a Tropical Institute in Germany, thinking that this was just a pro forma that travellers returning from the tropics should go through. Not in my wildest thoughts had I linked my previous swollen limbs and abdominal pains to any tropical disease, as I was convinced my inappropriate diet had caused these symptoms. However, the doctors told me otherwise. When I had eaten the Tilapia fish from the crater lake only partially cooked, I had also ingested parasites called liver flukes (*Chlonorchis sinensis*) that had caused all these health issues. Luckily, Ivo, who had regularly refused to eat the fish unless properly cooked, was spared. The tiny worms live in the bile duct between the liver and small intestines, and their presence explains why my body's immune system had cried out with rashes and pains and why I had trouble digesting fatty food. Bile is needed for such digestion, and the parasites block the pipe that delivers it. Many locals must also suffer from these parasites as they regularly consume Tilapia fish. We now remember that some of them consulted us about their gut issues, thinking that all white people are doctors.

During our stay, a local priest had proudly told us the story of how the Tilapia came to the island, probably the only relevant story of globalisation that has ever occurred on Niuafo'ou. These fish are not native to this island or any other place in Tonga but originated in Africa. They can be farmed quite easily and have thus been introduced to many areas of South-East Asia. Some decades ago, one Catholic priest who served his time on Niuafo'ou had also travelled to South-East Asia. He had brought with him a few Tilapia, hoping to complement the local menu by introducing them to the crater lake. Three of those fish had survived the arduous trip, reproduced quickly, and started a large population.

---

5. https://volcano.si.edu/showreport.cfm?doi=10.5479/si.GVP.BGVN200304-243110 and Paul Taylor, personal communication, March 2022

6. https://www.youtube.com/watch?v=gBpkYDppRtA

Our research into the lifecycle of liver flukes and Tilapia helped us establish what happened then. The fish had survived on algae and some native snails present in the lake. The parasites that entered the fish had reproduced equally fast but needed more help to stay alive. Like many parasites, they have a rather complicated reproductive cycle. While the adult flukes happily consume the juice in people's bile ducts, their eggs are passed into the stool. In the water, snails eat the eggs and are hosts for the larvae that hatch soon after. The larvae then float freely in the water before attaching themselves to a fish and borrowing into its flesh. People ingested the parasite when they ate Tilapia, which was either raw or not fully cooked. Here the cycle began again. No detective is needed to identify that this sequence required human faeces to somehow get into the water. As there were no toilets near the crater lake, one can only assume that this part of the cycle was completed by the locals who occasionally visited the lake to wash, fish, and dig for Malau eggs.

After my successful treatment with just one strong pill, we immediately wrote letters to Malohi and Kailao to warn them against eating the fish raw or partly cooked, as proper cooking destroys the parasite. We were hopeful that they would spread the word. My doctors at the Tropical Institute were surprised to find this parasite in someone coming from Tonga, and it took them weeks to detect it as they hadn't been searching for it. It is usually only known from South-East Asia, but the doctors weren't aware of the well-meaning intentions of that Catholic priest.

With plenty of data about the Malau to analyse, we both managed to complete our Master's degrees. As we had predicted, the Professor could not find anybody else to come to Tonga and continue with the translocation to Late. The equipment we left behind must have either fallen apart or, more likely, been used by Malohi and Kailao in many creative ways.

We continued to write letters back and forth with some of our Tongan friends for some years. These were so authentic that our minds were transported back to the island each time we read them. Laveni, for example, wrote that Malohi said "thank you very much" for the help we had provided to his family and that we were the good pālangi who had lived on Niuafo'ou and that now, only one pālangi was teaching at the High School. She also mentioned that it was much too cold when we were on the island, but it was warmer now, and she begged us to return. A new baby had been born but sadly had died soon after. Otherwise, she wrote that "the families on the island are good and happy." She also informed us that the plane and mail only arrived once a month, but they still had enough breadfruit. As is customary, she also asked whether Ivo was good or bad, whether he was the big fat or the small fat. In another letter, she wrote that "Ana and Ivo, you are beautiful small fat," so she had obviously finally accepted our slim appearance. Her letters always ended with lots of love from her family to my family and lots of prayers for us all, reflecting the Tongans' strong connections to family and church. My favourite line in one of her letters was this one: "Ana, enough of the letter, but not enough of the love."

Kailao, too, kept us in the loop and promised to spread the word about the parasite in the Tilapia fish. His letters focused on the education of his daughters. He was very proud of their excellent marks at the Tonga High School in Nuku'alofa, where they had to stay with relatives, away from their parents, to receive a better education than they would have received on Niuafo'ou. He also mentioned meetings of the island's elders in which they discussed the future of the Malau, and he informed us that he had written to the Tongan Ministry of Land, Survey and Natural Resources about protection measures for the birds. In one of his letters, he explained that he had long service leave coming up and hoped to spend it in Australia or the US, but then realistically declared that he might have to spend his holiday in his backyard due to the lack of pocket money.

We couldn't sponsor his long service leave overseas, but the letters from Niuafo'ou usually contained hints about which items our friends needed most. So we sent parcels with clothes, thongs, torches, a small manual camera and films for Laveni, handcuffs and sunglasses for Kailao, and lots of goodies for the kids. The parcels took three months via surface mail, but our friends were used to things arriving in Tongan Time. In return, Malohi's family sent us a beautiful large handwoven mat, which Emeni, Laveni, and others must have woven over weeks. They had produced most of it from dark-coloured pandanus leaves, but in the centre, they had intricately woven the name Niuafo'ou in a lighter colour. It was a work of art that could not be found anywhere else in Europe, that's for sure.

Ivo and I stayed together for another eleven years before we amicably went our separate ways. I ended up in Australia, where I studied a bird related to the Malau, the Australian Brush-turkey. Unfortunately, with our separation came the cessation of any letter contact with our friends in Tonga, for two reasons. First, it was not common on Niuafo'ou for couples to separate, and we did not want to share this news with them. Second, I did not want our friends to know that I now lived in Australia. For them, the biggest dream is to come to Australia, and if they have family there, they try every avenue to join them somehow. As Falaki and his family somewhat regarded me as part of their clan, this could have caused an awkward situation, as I was in no position to support any Tongan friends wanting to come and live with me.

With the arrival of the internet in my life, I was able to follow more reports about the island. A Peace Corps volunteer reported in 2011 that the island had one doctor, fuel for tractors was rare, and people still enjoyed Ofato[7]. A 2011 video on YouTube showed that disembarking on our island's rock platform was still tricky, but there were now more pickup trucks on Niuafo'ou[8]. In 2015, one adventurous traveller created a geocache on Motu Lahi, the largest of the islands in the crater lake[9]. His description of his travels wasn't much different from ours. For example, he warned that "you will most likely have to spend a considerable amount of time on Niuafo'ou due to flight and ferry schedules."

In 2016, the Tongan Red Cross donated 50 new water tanks[10], but this did not prevent a serious water shortage during an ongoing drought in 2021. A water desalination plant was donated to the island in 2021, providing several thousand litres of drinking water[11]. In 2018, the 'hospital' on the island was equipped with solar panels to provide lights 24/7, and not just 5 hours a day[12]. A 2020 report showed that the internet had reached three villages, but infrastructure, such as the road, was still in bad condition, partly due to a cyclone that made landfall in January 2020[13]. The runway for planes remained a grass strip, the road was partially blocked, and the locals couldn't afford the high fees for shipping goods to the island. Niuafo'ou High School had a Facebook page that was last used in 2018[14]. Students could also learn in a more modern building. Someone even donated a table tennis table to the school in 2020[15].

Also interesting to read was that the people of Niuafo'ou are regarded as some of the healthiest in Tonga, as they eat less imported food and more locally grown products[16]. I have experienced how much they love sipi—fatty mutton flaps—and corned beef. Due

---

7. http://atonganodyssey.blogspot.com/2011/09/niuafoou-you-will-never-go-here-pt5.html

8. https://www.youtube.com/watch?v=EJd1LgunNxo&t=4s&ab_channel=AndrewKot

9. https://www.geocaching.com/geocache/GC6BJBF_niuafoou?guid=82564f0d-f10b-4cb7-8b94-81674ac847ae

10. https://matangitonga.to/2016/01/20/new-water-tanks-niuafo-ou

11. https://reliefweb.int/sites/reliefweb.int/files/resources/Drought%20response%20in%20Niuatoputapu%20and%20Niaufo%E2%80%99ou%20%20%20Government%20of%20Tonga.pdf

12. https://www.pcreee.org/article/king-tupou-vi-commissions-first-solar-power-niuafo-ou-s-hospital

13. https://www.kanivatonga.nz/2020/02/pms-niuafoou-meeting-wharf-maintenance-roading-water-internet-ship-and-airline-charges-residents-main-concerns/

14. https://www.facebook.com/Niuafoou-high-school-471196799885275/

15. https://ittfoceania.com/2020/09/19/table-tennis-reaching-the-far-corners-of-tonga/

16. http://www.tonga-broadcasting.net/?p=8315

to the lack of supplies, they can't often obtain this fatty type of food. In contrast, rich and processed food has caused a huge obesity epidemic on other Tongan islands, with life expectancy continuously falling[17]. A 2016 scientific paper called Tonga the most obese country in the world[18]. While processed food is rare on Niuafo'ou, so is fresh fruit for visitors—which confirms our observations. Two young Peace Corps volunteers who stayed there from 2003 to 2005 suffered from scurvy, a disease caused by Vitamin C deficiency. They were the last volunteers to visit from that organisation, as the island was thereafter deemed too remote and too hard to reach[19].

I also wanted to know the fate of the rusty ferries we travelled on. No information was available on the Moana and Fokololo-oe Hau, but at least the Olovaha had officially been retired before it could sink. Sadly, it had been replaced with a rust bucket named Princess Ashika, which sank in 2009, killing 74 people on board. A Royal Commission of Inquiry found that this ship was never suited for Tongan waters and was in deplorable condition[20]. To us, this rang a bell, as none of the vessels we had travelled on seemed seaworthy either. Royal Tongan Airlines also had issues with its safety procedures. In 2001, it had to ground all of its planes due to inadequate maintenance procedures[21]. I am only glad we were unaware of any such issues in 1991 when travelling by air was the luxury mode of transportation compared to catching boats.

What was most important to establish was the status of the Malau and whether our translocation of eggs to Late Island did indeed result in a second population of Malau. Unfortunately, this is most likely not the case today, but it appears the birds initially survived. In 1994, two years after our last translocation, we received a letter from Salesi, the fisherman who took us to Late Island, in which he described holes in the ground that could have been Malau diggings. Here is the excerpt from his letter:

"In April, we went to Late and walked to the lake to watch the Malau. You know the path we walked to place the second eggs. I heard a voice like a Malau singing, and I saw that there were many holes dug near a big rock. These holes are very different from those made by rats or crabs; they are about 5 inches to 7 inches in diameter. I can show you a

---

17. https://www.bbc.com/news/magazine-35346493

18. https://www.thelancet.com/pdfs/journals/lancet/PIIS0140-6736(16)30054-X.pdf

19. https://www.friendsoftonga.org/cpages/evan-and-kate-buban-mangino/61f60d3596385f059945ff30

20. https://www.pressreader.com/new-zealand/the-press/20100102/283244504090569

21. https://openresearchrepository.anu.edu.au/bitstream/1885/157616/1/161_recent%20tonga.pdf

diagram (he added a drawing). Sorry, I cannot take a photo or make a tape because I didn't find this thing again. I think Malau is living at Late; I hope."

Also, in 1997, a French scientist and two Tongans working for the local zoo published a short report in which they claimed to have observed Malau on Late[22]. Two western scientists interviewed the German wife of one of those Tongans, who also said that the birds lived on Late, but they dismissed her account as containing too little 'hard evidence'[23].

We will never know for sure whether the birds survived for a while or not, and why scientists could not detect them in two short searches, lasting 2 and 4 days, in 2004[24] and 2013[25]. Perhaps not enough eggs hatched to start a large enough population. It could also be that Late's volcanic activity changed so that the Malau could no longer reach the warm soil for incubating, or the intense cyclone that hit the island in 2002 caused their extinction.

But at least a second population did become established on Fonualei. When Paul Taylor visited the island in 1998, he did not observe any Malau[26], but a special survey aimed at detecting the species found 56 adult Malau there in 2003[27]. This result reduces the species' chances of becoming extinct in the near future, although the volcano on active Fonualei is more likely to erupt than Late, and this would pose a threat to the survival of that new Malau population. Fresh lava flows were observed on the north-western side of this island's caldera, confirming a recent mini eruption[28].

---

22. Beaudry, J., Tutu'alao, F. and Matavalea, L. (1997). *Report on bird survey to Fonualei and Late, September-October 1996.* Unpublished report. Tongan Wildlife Centre, Tongatapu.

23. Watling, D. (2003). *Report on a Visit to* Late *and Fonualei Islands, Vava'u Group, Kingdom of Tonga.* Unpublished report to the Van Tienhoven Foundation. pp.19. https://pacificdata.org/data/dataset/report-on-a-visit-to-late-and-fonualei-islands-vavau-group-kingdom-of-tonga74833

24. Watling, D. (2004). No sign of translocated Polynesian megapodes on Late Island, Kingdom of Tonga. *Megapode Newsletter,* 18: 4.

25. Butler, D. (2013). *Bird Surveys of Late and Fonualei Islands, Vava'u, Kingdom of Tonga, September 2013.* Draft report. https://www.sprep.org/attachments/VirLib/Tonga/Tonga_bird-survey-Late-Fonualei-2013.pdf

26. Paul Taylor, personal communication, March 2022

27. Watling, D. (2003). *Report on a Visit to* Late *and Fonualei Islands, Vava'u Group, Kingdom of Tonga.* Unpublished report to the Van Tienhoven Foundation. pp.19. https://pacificdata.org/data/dataset/report-on-a-visit-to-late-and-fonualei-islands-vavau-group-kingdom-of-tonga74833

28. Paul Taylor, personal communication, March 2022.

On Niuafo'ou, the Malau is clinging to its home island, though its population has decreased and fewer eggs are being found. Our survey estimated a total number of between 188 and 235 adult Malau remaining on the island between 1991 and 1993[29].

Three groups of other researchers and representatives of the Tongan government visited Niuafo'ou for periods of 9 days to 4 weeks in 2010[30], 2012[31], and 2019[32]. With little time available, they could not repeat our detailed playback survey and thus did not estimate the number of Malau living there. Instead, they focused on the egg-laying grounds used by the birds. There were some inconsistencies in the definition of an 'active laying ground', as for an inexperienced observer, it is difficult to ascertain whether the birds have recently used a hole in the ground for egg-laying. But overall, all three surveys indicated a decline in active egg-laying burrows and thus a significant decrease in Malau numbers since we stayed on the island. The only consolation lies in a sentence in the report of the 2019 study, which states that 'Egg collection appears to be dying out as a tradition, and this may have led to the population stabilising at low levels since 2010'[33]. Also encouraging is a detailed community-based conservation plan that provides the Tongan people with substantial information about the Malau and the best measures to protect it from extinction[34]. Let's hope this bird will defy the odds and continue to inhabit its volcanic home for many more years to come.

---

29. Göth, A. et al. 1995. Status of the Polynesian Megapode *Megapodius pritchardii* on Niuafo'ou (Tonga). *Bird Conservation International* 5(01): 117-128.

30. Lloyd, H., Torres-Sovero, C. and Faka'osi, S. (2011). Conservation Strategy for the Polynesian megapode *Megapodius pritchardii* on Niuafo'ou, Tonga. *World Pheasant Association*, Newcastle UK and *Tonga Community Development Trust*, Tongatapu, Tonga. 41pp. https://www.researchgate.net/publication/321035246_Conservation_Strategy_for_the_Polynesian_Megapode_Megapodius_pritchardii_on_Niuafo'ou_Tonga

31. MLECCNR. (2012). *Report on a visit to Niuafo'ou Island, Kingdom of Tonga*. Unpublished report of Ministry of Lands, Environment, Climate Change and Natural Resources, Nuku'alofa, Tonga. 59 pp.

32. Butler, D.J. (2019). *Report on a visit to Niuafo'ou Island, Kingdom of Tonga*. Apia, Samoa: SPREB. ISBN 978-982-04-693-3. https://www.sprep.org/publications/report-on-a-visit-to-niuafoou-island-kingdom-of-tonga-polynesian-megapode-megapodius-pritchardii-monitoring-and-conservation-of-malau-on-niuafaoou-island

33. Same source as in last footnote.

34. Lloyd, H., Torres-Sovero, C. and Faka'osi, S. (2011). See details above.

Afterthought. Life in Tonga Under Climate Change

A picture of islands being flooded by rising seawaters is what most people have in mind when thinking about the impacts of climate change in the South Pacific. My trip to Tonga has made me aware that there is more to this issue, and that the people and nature in Tonga are dealing with wider-reaching impacts lesser-known to many. It is correct that low-lying coral islands are already threatened by rising sea levels and need to adapt. This also applies to the coral islands we visited: Tongatapu, Kotu, Lifuka, Hunga, and islands in the Vava'u group. Approximately 80% of Tongans live on coral islands right on the coast[1]. But even if they haven't been flooded yet, people and wildlife on these islands suffer from the changes in soil composition, which affect the number and types of crops humans can grow and the types of plants wildlife can feed and live on. Through a process called saltwater intrusion, salt enters the soil when seawater permeates the soil from underneath and around the islands. As the sea level rises, so does the amount of salt that manages to find its way into the soil, especially on smaller islands. Not many plants grow in salty soil!

Islands that haven't been flooded yet are gradually becoming smaller, making it harder to sustain the people living on them. Each time a large storm or cyclone hits, the shore is eroded, washing coconut palms and other vegetation into the sea. Even before the 2022 tsunami, the manager of a tourist resort on the small island of Fafa in Tonga thought that it was unlikely his island would still exist in 100 years and had already started moving his buildings further back from the shore. Additionally, a road on Tongatapu has been

---

1. https://www.bbc.com/news/business-34738408

washed away by the rising tides, and an uninhabited island that locals used for fishing is now barely visible above the water level[2].

Climate change will also intensify extreme weather events, such as storms, cyclones, heatwaves, and droughts, and it may change rainfall patterns[3]. Tonga has no streams or freshwater lakes, so rainfall is crucial for its water supply. People depend on rainwater caught on rooftops and stored in cisterns. Only a few larger islands have a thin lens of freshwater located in the porous limestone ground, but this too is threatened by saltwater intrusion. It is easy to envisage the effects of altered rainfall patterns on drinking water supplies and the ability to grow plants and food. Authorities predict with high confidence that Small Island Developing States, like Tonga, will experience freshwater shortages when droughts occur as a result of climate change[4].

The reefs surrounding coral islands also suffer from climate change. Corals break off during cyclones, and they bleach when the water becomes too hot. Without corals, most other species in the reef cannot survive. Seafood from those reefs is often the most critical source of food for coral islanders. Even when I was visiting 30 years ago, the reefs were showing signs of overharvesting and destruction of corals by people breaking them. Other countries now apply methods such as coral and mangrove planting, but to my knowledge, this is not yet often done in Tonga.

Volcanic islands like Niuafo'ou are higher and less likely to be impacted by rising seawater levels. However, they too are likely to suffer from various impacts predicted by the Intergovernmental Panel on Climate Change (IPCC)[5]. One of these is the impact on water scarcity, as these islands rely heavily on rainwater for drinking and growing crops. Water cannot be shipped in easily due to their remoteness. This makes droughts a serious threat to all inhabitants. Being so remote also makes these islands more vulnerable to being cut off from supplies during periods of extreme weather. Supply ships or planes already visit Niuafo'ou very infrequently, and any further decrease in the provisioning of food and materials makes survival on this island harder. It also means the locals rely more on the natural resources on their home island, and unfortunately, the eggs of the Malau are one of these.

---

2. Same source as last footnote.

3. https://www.sprep.org/attachments/Publications/FactSheet/pacificclimate.pdf

4. https://report.ipcc.ch/ar6wg2/pdf/IPCC_AR6_WGII_FactSheet_SmallIslands.pdf

5. https://www.ipcc.ch/report/ar6/wg2/

Tropical cyclones are not only a direct threat to people and livestock, but they also destroy the crops that people rely on. A 1982 cyclone blew 95% of all ripening coconuts as well as 90% of breadfruit and bananas throughout all of Tonga's islands from the trees, thus seriously depleting food resources for the locals[6]. On Niuafo'ou and other remote islands, people suffer even more when such depletion of food resources is combined with the destruction of infrastructure and an absence of supplies from outside.

While the Kingdom of Tonga consists of 171 named islands, only 36 of them are permanently inhabited[7]. This means that the 107,000 people inhabiting Tonga today[8] depend on the infrastructure established on relatively few islands. Hence, the observed impacts of climate change affect a disproportionately high number of people. In addition, severe weather events exacerbated by climate change increase the risk of diseases due to higher temperatures, more flooding, and contaminated water. Dengue fever did not seem to be present when we lived in Tonga, but in 2003, an outbreak occurred that resulted in several deaths[9].

It is not easy to end this book on a depressing note, but increased awareness is the first step towards change and taking this crisis seriously. We need to listen to the recent United Nations climate change report[10], which demonstrates the intensifying effects of climate change, and we need to believe that we can still turn this around. I conclude with a quote from Will Turner, senior scientist at Conservation International: "At this point, inaction due to uncertainty is scientifically unjustifiable, and inaction due to hopelessness is indefensible. We can still make a difference, but we must act now"[11]. Apart from the contribution that each of us can make, small island nations like Tonga will benefit from

---

6. Mimura, N. and Pelesikoti, N. (1997). 'Vulnerability of Tonga to future sea-level rise', *Journal of Coastal Research*, 24: 117-132.

7. Same source as last footnote.

8. https://www.worldometers.info/world-population/tonga-population/

9. https://www.pphsn.net/Private/Dengue_in_Tonga-Summary_with_graph.pdf

10. https://www.ipcc.ch/report/ar6/wg1/

11. https://www.conservation.org/blog/don%E2%80%99t-panic-reasons-for-hope-despite-a-grim-un-climate-report

the continuation of existing programmes that focus on building resilience to climate change[12]. These nations, including Tonga, have now become a strong voice in the United Nations Climate Change Conferences (COP), and it is good to see the international community listening more to their concerns.

---

12. https://www.adb.org/countries/tonga/main and https://projects.worldbank.org/en/projects-operations/project-detail/P161539 and https://www.theprif.org/sites/default/files/documents/PRIF_SLR-Report_Digital_0.pdf
https://unfccc.int/sites/default/files/resource/TONGA_cop26cmp16cma3_HLS_EN.pdf

Acknowledgements

A big thank you to all the people in Tonga, especially on Niuafo'ou, who helped us during our stay in one way or another and introduced us to A*nga Faka-Tongá*—the Tongan way of life. I can't name these people individually for privacy reasons, but I hope they know who they are and still remember me fondly as Ana Malau after all these years.

This expedition wouldn't have been possible without my boyfriend, named Ivo in this book. We were a great team, and I thank him for his substantial contributions to our survival on the islands, my personal growth, our scientific discoveries, and our conservation efforts for the Malau. Even though we eventually went our separate ways, I greatly appreciate that he supported me in every possible way.

I am also forever grateful to the many organisations and individuals who financed this expedition: The Dr Otto Röhm Gedächtnisstiftung, Deutsche Ornithologen-Gesellschaft, Gesellschaft für Tropenornithologie, Vereinigung für Artenschutz, Vogelhaltung und Vogelzucht, World PheasantAssociation, Dr Erichsen, E. Fromme, Dr Jungbecker, Dr Müller, Mr Nicolson, and my dear late grandfather, Ernst Trommsdorff.

Thank you to my parents, who always believed in me and gave me the freedom and support to study what I loved—biology, especially conservation biology. They probably didn't expect me to venture to the other side of the Earth at the age of 21, but they knew they couldn't stop me, even if they had tried. My mum, Christl, diligently typed up all the letters I sent home, which I later based this book on.

Writing a book of this type was a new experience, and many people helped me improve my writing along the way. Lliane Clarke's encouragement as a manuscript assessor was infectious, and so was the feedback I received from my writer's group, especially Christine Williams from the Sydney School of Art and Humanities, who also edited some chapters for me. I am grateful to my husband, Wayne, and friends who commented on earlier drafts of this book and considerably helped improve it in whole or in part, in particular, Annett Naumann, Cath and Robert Kench, and René Dekker. Members of the Facebook Group "We Love Memoirs" kindly provided valuable advice during the preparation of this reprint of the book.

Two specialists in their fields kindly ensured that I got my facts right: Sandra Schuster checked my chapter on climate change, and Paul Taylor approved all my wording related to volcanology. I am also grateful to Paul for providing two of the maps included.

And last but not least, thank you to the members of the World Pheasant Association/Megapode Specialist Group, especially René Dekker and Darryl Jones. They supported me by believing in my work and making me feel like it was all worthwhile, especially during difficult times. Darryl also enabled me to continue working with this fascinating group of birds and turn my passion for megapode chicks into a higher degree in Australia. It was a journey I would not want to have missed!

Maps

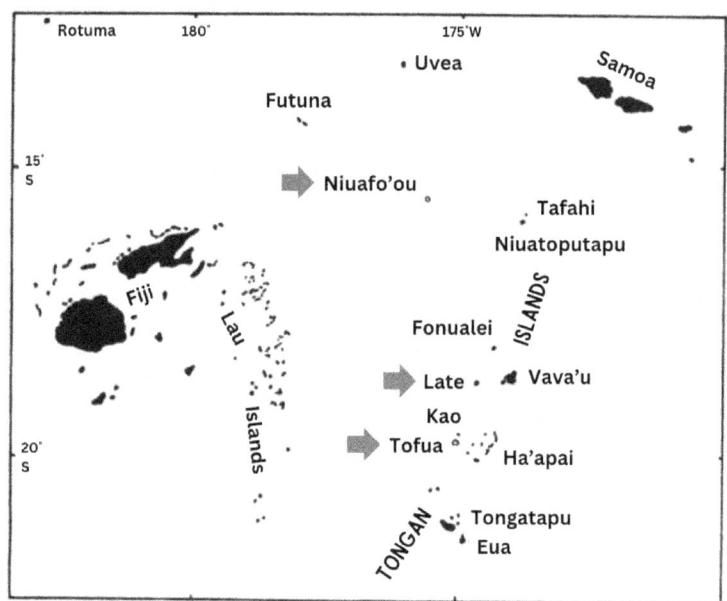

Map 1. Map of the Southwest Pacific region showing the location of Niuafo'ou and the volcanoes Late and Tofua (which we visited) as well as Fonualei (which we didn't visit). See Maps 3 and 4 for further islands we visited in the Vava'u and Ha'apai groups of islands. Map courtesy of Paul Taylor.

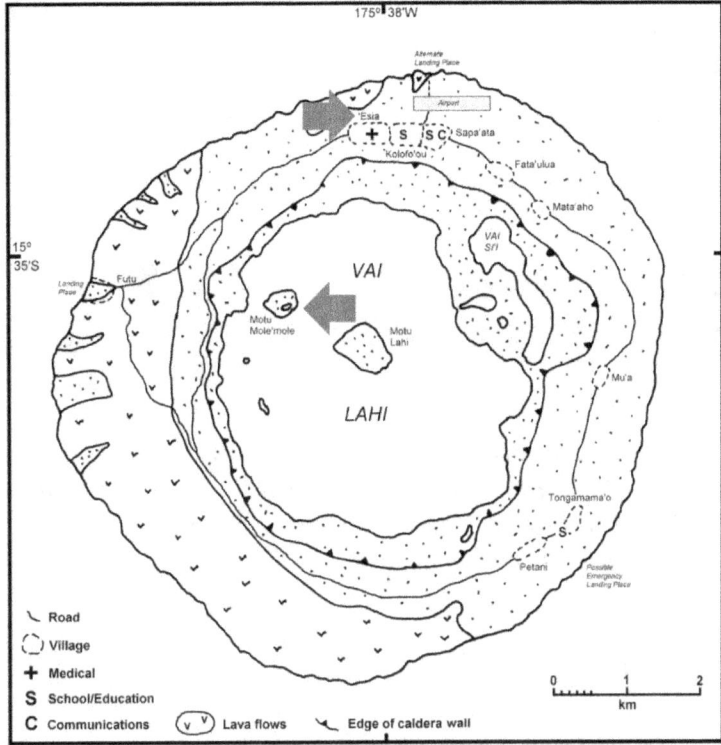

Map 2. The volcano Niuafo'ou. The arrows indicate the village where we stayed (Esia) and the islet where we camped (Motu Molemole). Map courtesy of Paul Taylor.

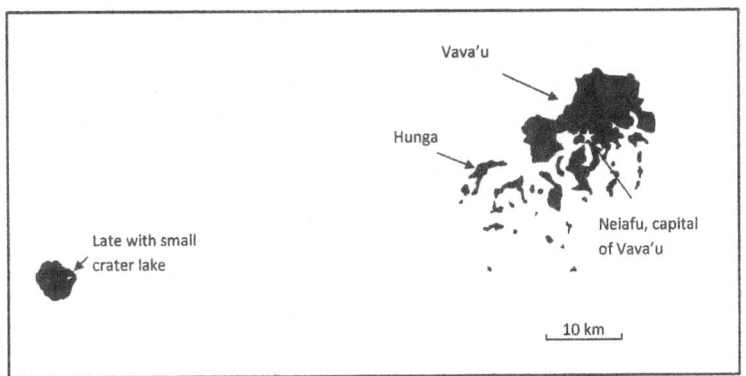

Map 3. The Vava'u Group with the Hunga coral island we visited while travelling to the volcano Late.

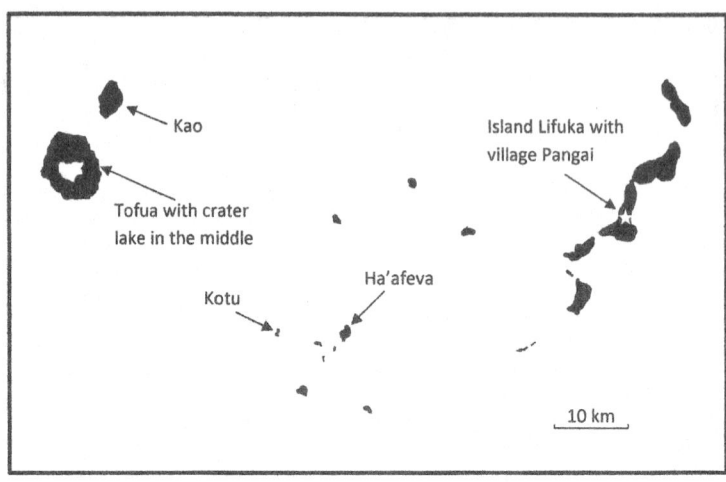

Map 4. The Ha'apai Group with the coral islands we visited while travelling to the volcano Tofua. Note: We did not visit Kao, but it features in the book as the island near where the mutiny of the Bounty occurred.

Places, Names and Tongan Words

The places

Esia	our village on Niuafo'ou
Fonualei	a small volcanic island we did not visit
Ha'afeva	a coral island east of *Kotu* where we first anchored
Ha'apai	a large group of islands between the capital and *Vava'u*
Hunga	a coral island in the *Vava'u* group, from where we left for Late. This is a different island to the one named Hunga Tonga—Hunga Ha'apai that violently erupted in January 2022.
Kotu	a small coral island in *Ha'apai* from where we ventured to Tofua
Kao	a volcanic cone near where the Mutiny of the Bounty occurred
Late	a larger volcanic island we visited
Lifuka	the largest coral island in the *Ha'apai* group
Motu molemole	an islet in the crater lake of Niuafo'ou where we often camped
Neiafu	the capital of *Vava'u*
Niuafo'ou	our remote island—Tin Can Island
Niuatoputapu	the remote sister island to Niuafo'ou
Nuku'alofa	the capital of Tonga on the island of *Tongatapu*
Pangai	the largest settlement on *Lifuka*
Tofua	a larger volcanic island we visited
Tongatapu	the main coral island containing the capital *Nuku'alofa*
Vava'u	a large island group halfway between *Tongatapu* and Niuafo'ou

The people

Ivo	my boyfriend and partner on this expedition
The Professor	Ivo's supervisor at a German University and our supervisor in this project

On Niuafo'ou

Malohi	local chief and our host
Emeni	Malohi's wife
Kailao	the police officer
Laaka	Malohi's adult daughter
Laveni	Malohi's teenage daughter
Lakepi	Malohi's adult son; expert in digging up Malau eggs
Laione	a local man who hosted the researcher David Todd
Salesi	the bank and post officer
Tokoni	our helper when building traps for the Malau
Werner	an Austrian from Vava'u who visited in his seaplane

On Kotu and Tofua

Afah	a fisherman from Kotu who took us to Tofua
Langi	Afah's sister, a dignified local leader
Tavite	a local guide from Kotu who assisted us on Tofua
Tokoni	a man who lived on Tofua and helped us a lot

On Vava'u

Tāufa'āhau Tupou IV	His Excellency, the King of Tonga
Rolf	an Austrian who has lived here for many years and established a guest house and several businesses
Lautoka	Rolf's Tongan wife

On Hunga and Late

Salesi	a local fisherman from Hunga who took us to Late Island
Vaha	a second fisherman from Hunga who assisted on Late Island

In Nuku'alofa

Mr Hopps	the German manager of a zoo in Tonga, the second supervisor in this project
Mr Consul	the German consul in Tonga
Susan	Mr Hopps's wife
Haniteli	an employee of Mr Hopps
Langi	a friend of Rolf who helped me when I had to solve visa issues

The ships

Moana	The vessel we first travelled on, from Nuku'alofa to Niuafo'ou. The Tongan word *moana* means ocean.
Fokololo-oe Hau	A rusty vessel that transported our goods from Vava'u to Niuafo'ou; also dubbed 'the swimming coffin' by the Tongans.
Olovaha	A larger car ferry that carried us from Ha'apai to Vava'u.

Some Tongan words and phrases often used

Ko ho'o 'alú ki fē?	Where are you going?
'Alu ai	You go there
Anga Faka-Tongá	The traditional Tongan way
Anga Faka-Pālangi	The Western way
Ceke	Pancakes made of flour and water and deep-fried in tallow
Fiekaia	hungry
'Io	Yes
Kava	A local drink made from the chewed leaves of the kava bush, with sedative and anaesthetic properties similar to alcohol.
Kiekie	A decorative waistband of woven strips of pandanus
Lelei 'aupito	Very good
Lotu	A church
Malo	Thank you
Malo e lelei	Hello, good day
Pa'anga	The Tongan currency
Pālangi	All white people
Sipi	Flaps of New Zealand mutton preserved in salt brine and sold in buckets
Tapa	A fabric made of the inner bark of a mulberry tree
Ta'ovala	A woven skirt made of the leaves of the Pandanus or *Fanakio* tree
Talitali fiefia	Welcome
Tapu	Taboo
Tevolo	The devil
Toi pe tapaka?	Do you have tobacco?
Umu	An earth oven

About the author

Dr Ann Göth is an ecologist, high school teacher, public speaker and passionate writer. Her writing reflects a strong passion to bring natural history and conservation issues closer to non-scientists and scientists alike. This book is a vivid account of her very first adventure as a conservation ecologist. Her career has taken her from Austria to islands in Tonga, the UN in Geneva and to universities, government agencies and schools in Australia. She now lives in Sydney, Australia, with her husband and son.

Her other books are **'Moundbuilders'** (about megapode birds in Australia; CSIRO Publishing, 2008), **'Amazing Annoying Birds'** (all about Australian brush-turkeys, Natural Publishing, 2023) and **'Bush-turkey Needs a Friend'** (an illustrated children's book about Australian brush-turkeys, Natural Publishing, 2023).

Find out more on Ann's website: https://anngothauthor.com

Thank you for reading my book! I am grateful and hope you found value in it. Please consider sharing it with family or friends and leaving a review online, as this would be very valuable in my quest to promote this book to a wider readership.

Further Reading

Tonga and Niuafo'ou

Advameg. (2016). Tonga. Countries and their Cultures. http://www.everyculture.com/To-Z/Tonga.html

Bennett, S. N., Plant, H. and Boekweg, M. (2017). *Tongan Culture.*

Garth, R. (Ed.). (1986). *The Fire has Jumped—Eye witness accounts of the eruption and evacuation of Niuafo'ou, Tonga.* Suva, Fiji: University of the South Pacific, Institute of Pacific Studies.

Göth, A. and Vogel, U. (1999). Notes on breeding and conservation of birds on Niuafo'ou Island, Kingdom of Tonga. *Pacific Conservation Biology*, 5: 103-115.

Herda, P., Terrell, J. and Gunson, N. (Eds). (1987). *Tongan culture and history: papers from the 1st Tongan History Conference held in Canberra, 14-17 January 1987.* Canberra: Dept. of Pacific and Southeast Asian History, Australian National University, 1990.

Jaggar, T. (1931). Geology and geography of Niuafo'ou Volcano. *Volcano letter*, 318: 1-3.

Safari the Globe. (2014). *Tonga.*

Shumway, E.B. (1988). *Intensive Course in Tongan.* Institute for Polynesian Studies, Brigham Young University, Hawaii. Revised edition. 783 pp.

Stanley, D. (2000). *South Pacific Handbook.* Avalon Travel Publishing; 7th edition (20 January 2000), 950 pp.

Venzke, E. (Ed). (2003). Report on Niuafo'ou (Tonga). *Bulletin of the Global Volcanism Network*, 28: 4. Smithsonian Institution.https://volcano.si.edu/showreport.cfm?doi=10.5479/si.GVP.BGVN200304-243110

The Malau and megapode birds

Butler, D.J. (2019). *Report on a visit to Niuafo'ou Island, Kingdom of Tonga.* Apia, Samoa: SPREB. ISBN 978-982-04-693-3

Booth, D.T. and Jones, D.N. (2002). Underground nesting in megapodes. In *Avian Incubation: Behaviour, Environment, and Evolution.* (Ed. DC Deeming). pp. 192-206. Oxford: Oxford University Press.

Göth, A. (1993). Status des Polynesischen Grossfusshuhns auf der Insel Niuafo'ou. *Journal für Ornithologie*, 135: 641-642

Göth, A. and Vogel, U. (1995). Status of the Polynesian Megapode *Megapodius pritchardii* on Niuafo'ou (Tonga). *Bird Conservation International*, 5: 117-128.

Göth, A., Vogel, U. and Curio, E. (1999). The acoustic communication of the Polynesian Megapode. *Zoologische Verhandelingen, Leiden*, 327: 37-51.

Göth, A. and Vogel, U. (2004). Is monogamy in the Polynesian megapode related to its high relative egg-weight? *The Auk*, 121: 308-317

Jones, D.N., Dekker, R.W.R.J. and Roselaar, C.S. (1995). *The Megapodes.* Oxford, UK: Oxford University Press. 262pp.

Jones, D.N. and Göth, A. (2008). *Mound-builders.* Collingwood, Victoria: CSIRO Publishing. 119 pp.

Lloyd, H., Torres-Sovero, C. and Faka'osi, S. (2011). Conservation Strategy for the Polynesian megapode *Megapodius pritchardii* on Niuafo'ou, Tonga. *World Pheasant Association*, Newcastle UK and *Tonga Community Development Trust*, Tongatapu, Tonga. 41 pp.

Rinke, D. (1986). Notes on the avifauna of Niuafo'ou Island, Kingdom of Tonga. *Emu*, 86: 82-86.

Rinke, D. (1991). Birds of Ata and Late and additional notes on the avifauna on Niuafo'ou, Kingdom of Tonga. *Notornis*, 38: 131-151.

Rinke, D. (1994). The Malau on Fonualei in northern Tonga. *World Pheasant Association News*, 44, 7-8.

Seymour, R.S. and Ackermann, R.A. (1980). Adaptations to underground nesting in birds and reptiles. *American Zoologist*, 20: 437-447.

Todd, D.M. (1983). Pritchard's megapode on Niuafo'ou Island, Kingdom of Tonga. *World Pheasant Association Journal*, 8: 69-88.

Watling, D. (1982). *Birds of Fiji, Tonga and Samoa.* Wellington, NZ: Millwood Press.

Weir, D.G. (1973). Status and habits of *Megapodius pritchardii*. Wilson Bulletin, 85: 79-82.

Malau scratching for food

www.ingramcontent.com/pod-product-compliance
Lightning Source LLC
Chambersburg PA
CBHW072003290426
44109CB00018B/2114